RURAL JAPAN

*Happy anniversary
with gratitude for
each ordinary moment —
Love,
Re*

June 19, 1992

RURAL JAPAN

LINDA BUTLER

RADIANCE OF THE ORDINARY

Foreword by Donald Richie

Smithsonian Institution Press   Washington and London

Haiku translation © 1992 by Jonathan
    Greene
Calligraphy by Keishō Ōkubo
Acquisitions editor, Amy Pastan
Editing by Lorraine L. Atherton
Production editing by Jack Kirshbaum
Cover photograph: *Backlit Radishes* by
    Linda Butler
Dust jacket photograph of author:
    Bryan Baylor

Library of Congress Cataloging-in-
Publication Data
Butler, Linda
    Rural Japan : radiance of the ordinary
/ photographs and text by Linda Butler.
    p.   cm. ISBN 1-56098-116-4 (cloth);
1-56098-141-5 (paper)   1. Country
life — Japan.   2. Country life —
Japan — Pictorial works.   I. Title.
DS811.B87   1991
952.04″ — dc20   91-17090
                                            CIP

The paper used in this publication meets
the minimum requirements of the
American National Standard for
Permanence of Paper for Printed Library
Materials Z39.48-1984
    For permission to reproduce
illustrations appearing in this book,
please correspond directly with the
author. The Smithsonian Institution
Press does not retain reproduction rights
for these illustrations or maintain a file
of addresses for photo sources.

For Steve

Foreword

To journey into the country, away from the city, is to travel in time as well. Deep in the mountains of Iwate, among the Yamagata paddies, on the coastal plain of Shimane, we are a full century away from the towers of Tokyo. Here we travel a neglected path, one that leads back to the remains of traditional Japan — not the mummified remnants of Kyoto nor the gentrifications of Kurashiki, but the mundane still-lives, still living in their ordinary radiance, of a hamlet off the highway, a forgotten fishing port, a country crossroads.

In rural Japan we can begin to sense age, patina, the sheen of use. Here, when listened to, things speak of age; objects handled by generations, when regarded, indicate authority. Kitchen pots in flat, dark Shiga are supremely themselves — the mirror of metal, the grain of wood, the shine of lacquer — eloquent survivors (plate 3).

Things lost in time here in the backcountry assert an individuality that is based upon endurance. Even new pots in old shapes hold this accent of authority (plate 26); basins, so similar in shape, share a dialect (plate 31); old brooms against a clay wall confidently speak of the shape of the plants beneath (plate 44); and a section of a *tokonoma* alcove tells the story of a time when wood, respected, was worked for sheen, where its reflections created a world of accord, a time when congruity created reflections of compliance, never noticed because so natural (plate 10). There are many such linkages in this spontaneous rural world. A pagoda stands in a snowy wood, and beside it stand those natural pagodas, the trees (plate 5). The result is not metaphor. It is correspondence.

Such correspondences have been noted. In fact, names have been given. One of them is haiku, a term indicating that line of measured prose that draws attention to the correspondence. Sometimes what catches the eye is cause and effect: in the spring rain, drops caught on the trees are blossoms (plate 17). Sometimes it is analogy: that snow-covered roof is a mountain until you see the ridgepole (plate 57).

This sage glance, this placid penetration, we expect from a kimonoed poet, brush in hand. We do not expect it from someone with a camera, someone foreign to Japan at that. Yet, the poetic urge is universal, the haiku shares with all lyric verse, and — as many poets have themselves told us — perhaps it is unfamiliarity that allows one finally to see.

Linda Butler looks into her viewfinder and sees that the pots for the tea water have not only their own shape but also their own weight (plate 48), that carp are also swimming in the sky (plate 27), that there is a common and visible correspondence between the winter-wet paddy and its extension, the spring-shrouded farmhouse in the distance (plate 7). Many of the things seen are as mysterious to her as they are to us. Sea urchins? Shaving brushes? No — ordered tea whisks in a box (plate 49). Living limbs against the sky? Some fabled tubular tree? Not at all — radishes against the light (plate 45). For her, things are seen at first sight, which, like first love, is all innocence. Hers too is an eye freed from the grime of habit, freed to see afresh, to complete the sentence that the scene began, now fit within the frame of the finished print.

Back from the land where time casts yet its long shadow, where the natural correspondence is still to be observed, the photograph completes its natural magic. It too returns to its source: the ordering of congruity, the creation of the paradigm.

There sits Hotei, bald pate, fat belly, robes in disarray, come all the way from China but now for a long time as Japanese as anyone (plate 12). Ancient, he still sits there, but now his lacquer peels like long dead skin, exposing the smooth bones of the round wood beneath. Ancient but still alive. For there, in front of him, stand, in tribute, fresh flowers.

Donald Richie

The combined energy and commitment of more than a hundred people on both sides of the Pacific have helped to create this book. Even though it is impossible to thank individually everyone who aided me in this project, I am grateful for the friendship and encouragement offered to me.

I was introduced to Japan in 1967 by Jackson Bailey, who established the Japan Study Program at Earlham College, Richmond, Indiana. Three other Earlham faculty, Akiko and Mitsuo Kakutani and Len Holvik, encouraged my interest in the language and arts of Japan. All four provided essential advice and support from 1986 to 1991, during my exploration of rural Japan and my preparation of the manuscript.

In 1968, the staff of Ichibaku-ryō, in Shiga prefecture, welcomed me as a volunteer at a retarded children's home. The director, Ichiji Tamura, opened his personal vision of Japanese culture to me through his paintings and proverbs. Kisayo and Ikuo Itō have included me in their home as if I were a member of their family. Fusa Itoga, Shigeno Ishihara, Mieko Tamura, and the families of Junichi Takeuchi, Taichi Yoshinaga, and Hiroyoshi Kosako have generously shared their time with me, providing a community of trusted friends.

I discovered the beauty of Iwate prefecture through the assistance of former mayor Kojirō Seki and his wife and the Ishidoriya Board of Education. Eietsu Fujita and his family welcomed me as a frequent visitor to their farm. Their openness and support were of immeasurable importance to this project. My affection for Yamagata prefecture was inspired by relationships with Nasuko and Yoshihiko Yamaguchi and Aya and Aki Kurimoto. I enjoyed the jaunts through the countryside with Japanese photographer Eiichi Saitō.

In Shimane prefecture, Masaki Maeda and his family provided warm hospitality and crucial support. In Nagasaki prefecture, I appreciated the generosity of Mr. and Mrs. Kashizō Watanabe; in Aichi prefecture, of Hitoshi Yokokume and Morii Taira; and in Aomori prefecture, of Harue Tsubota. In Tokyo, the staff at International House of Japan — Mikio Katō, Tomiyo Togasaki, Izumi Koide, and Tatsuo Tanami — offered guidance.

Friendships with several Japanese living in Kentucky encouraged my

Acknowledgments

renewed association with Japan. Keiko Saitō, Hiroko Ochiai, and Miyuki Mizoguchi were tireless resources; they investigated my questions and assisted with translation and correspondence. I am also grateful to Yoshimi Fukuda, Ryoko Marlin, Atsuko Takami, and Takako Ioku for their assistance.

The initial writing of the text was done with the support and thoughtful editing of Judy Young and Jane Wilson Joyce. My sister, Sandra Nakamura, also provided editorial suggestions. Keiko Sawaragi, a contemporary Japanese poet, wrote haiku to accompany several of the photographs. Early in the project, Liza Dalby and Betsey Scheiner counseled me on thematic directions. Carolyn Hisel and Nancy Medwell offered honest critiques of the photographs; George Ella Lyon, Audrey Robinson, and Jane Gentry Vance made suggestions regarding the text. The Kentucky Arts Council, the Kentucky Foundation for Women, and the Nomura Cultural Foundation furnished grants for which I am deeply appreciative.

I am grateful to the staff of the Smithsonian Institution Press for their commitment to publish this work. My particular thanks go to Amy Pastan, whose energy and decisiveness kept this project focused; to Jack Kirshbaum and Lorraine Atherton, whose editing enhanced the manuscript; to Janice Wheeler, who created the elegant design; and to Kathleen Brown, who assured the high-quality production. I would like to thank Donald Richie for his poetic foreword and Keishō Ōkubo for her calligraphy. My gratitude to Robert J. Smith and Miwa Kai, whose bilingual abilities aided this project; to Jonathan Greene, who translated the haiku; and to Bryan Baylor, who assisted me in the preparation of the prints.

Finally, I appreciate the endurance of my husband, Steven Nissen. His support allowed my vision to become a reality.

RURAL JAPAN

*A*t noon the Fujitas' grandmother asked me to take a break from my photography to join her family for lunch. She was planning to serve a rural delicacy that is now rarely eaten by the Japanese. In the kitchen, she placed a two-inch cube of tofu (bean curd) and several small, live eels at the center of lacquer bowls. Just before the soup was served, she poured soup stock into each bowl. To escape the heat, the eels plunged into the cool tofu and smothered.

In the formal dining room we knelt around a lacquer table. The fifty-year-old Mr. Fujita sat at the head of the table. Outside the sliding screens was a carefully composed rock garden, but it was the fifteen-inch-long white radishes drying in the cool fall air that captured my attention. Just as the soup arrived, there was a break in the clouds and the sun came out. The radishes were transformed — looking almost translucent. I knew I had to act quickly to capture this image, so I excused myself in the polite language customarily used by Japanese in formal situations. It took me ten minutes to set up the camera and expose a negative. When I returned to lunch, my soup was lukewarm and the eels seemed particularly dead, but the image of the radishes (plate 45) would become the beginning of my photographic work in rural Japan.

*M*y association with the Japanese began in 1967 when, as a college student, I lived in Japan for a year. I was awed by the experience of discovering a new culture. On my first day in Tokyo, I purchased a camera and recorded my experiences for the succeeding twelve months. In addition to studying language and culture in Tokyo, I spent three months working as a volunteer at a home for retarded children not far from Kyoto. On morning walks through the rural countryside I observed the local farmers hanging winter vegetables from bamboo poles in orderly rows. Several of the staff members took time to introduce me to various aspects of Japanese culture. One taught me folk songs, another proverbs. On days off, staff members guided me on trips to back-country kilns and temples. Since no one could afford a car, we traveled by bus or train, or we hiked.

"Out of nothingness, something is born." (Mu kara yū o umu.)

In February, several of us were caught in a snowstorm on a large hill outside Ōtsu. The wet snow stuck to the pine and cedar trees. As we came down the mountain, we saw the city transformed into a silent monochromatic world. Cars and electrical lines were concealed under a quilt of whiteness. We gazed at the pattern of the tile rooftops and the stark black wood of a local shrine. I felt as if I had stepped into a hundred-year-old black and white woodblock print.

My aesthetic preferences were forever altered during those months, but when I boarded the plane that took me back to the United States, I assumed my connection with Japan was over. At home in Wisconsin, as I packed to return to college, I stored the namecards of my friends and acquaintances in a small, black book and my photographs neatly in a red lacquer box. Although I carried these two objects with me through seventeen moves in the next nineteen years, I never opened them. I traded my camera for a motor scooter and postponed work in photography for a decade.

Nearly twenty years after my first exposure to Japan, employees of Japanese companies began to appear near my home in central Kentucky during the construction of a Toyota automobile assembly plant. With the help of those families, I reestablished my association with Japan. I again studied the Japanese language and made a decision to return.

Japan had changed dramatically in the years between 1967 and 1986. In comparison with the backward villages I remembered, now even rural towns have a modern luster. Most families own at least one car, so even the downtowns of rural cities are crowded with traffic. In 1967 there was no money for extras. Now the main streets bustle with adult shoppers and with children buying candy and video games.

Just under the surface, however, the ancient rural culture still exists. Young people who choose to return to their hometowns after graduating from universities in Tokyo or Osaka sometimes complain of the feudalistic rules that govern rural relationships. Rural people may have discarded their kimonos for western clothes, but the customs that governed Japan for centuries have an astonishing resilience.

City dwellers are embarrassed by the unsophisticated nature of life in rural areas and would prefer to show foreigners the modern advances, not the *ura* (back side) of their culture. Many of the younger generation choose to work in the cities, far away from their parents and relatives. They take jobs in leading companies and enjoy the stimulation — the discos, movies, and active nightlife — of big-city living. Rural customs, however, continue to influence how people interact even in the cities. Many of the basic rules of etiquette and themes that govern lives — issues of obligation, hierarchy, and loyalty — are surprisingly similar in industrial and rural Japan.

After returning from Japan, I spent the next month in the darkroom. Eventually, I discarded both excessively sentimental photographs of traditional scenes and overly documentary interpretations of rural life. From the entire trip, only five prints possessed the combination of originality and spiritual presence that I was seeking (plates 44, 45, 46, 48, 54). They became the foundation of a new body of work. During the next two years, I would make four additional trips to Japan, attempting to capture the spirit of each of the four seasons.

A Japanese woman living in Kentucky who saw me struggling with the early conceptualization of my project taught me a Japanese proverb that relates to the creative process. "Mu kara yū o umu" ("Out of nothingness, something is born"). She added the word "taihen!" ("difficult").

*I*n fall 1986, I met the Fujita family almost totally by chance. An American professor of Japanese history introduced me to the mayor of Ishido-riya, a small town in Iwate-ken (the prefecture of Iwate) in northern Japan. The mayor asked the assistant superintendent of schools to escort me on a day of photographic sightseeing.

"Do good things quickly."
(Zen wa isoge.)

As part of our itinerary, I asked to see a thatched-roof house, since they are becoming rare. Late in the day, we drove along a river to see a two-hundred-year-old home east of town.

We arrived behind schedule and the owner was not at home. Fifteen minutes later she ran up the driveway, flustered by our presence in her yard. She apologized to the assistant superintendent because she didn't have time to show us the inside of her house. Unexpectedly, she had been hired by her neighbors — the Fujitas — to harvest rice. I asked if we might follow her to watch the process.

Ten people were assisting the Fujita family that afternoon. The women carried bundles of rice stalks from the fields where they had been drying for a month. Mr. Fujita and a hired man fed the rice into a threshing machine, which separated the grain from the stalks. During lulls, Mr. Fujita shouted above the noise of the machine to inquire about the purpose of my photography. His mother, breaking away from the group of women, listened intently. Soon we were invited to join the family for late afternoon tea.

Grandmother Fujita beckoned me to follow her into the house — through a wrought iron gate, past piles of enormous rocks saved for future rock gardens, past turkeys and chickens running skittishly to avoid us, past a deer in a cage, a cow in a shed, and a fish carcass drying under the eaves. Ducking under fishing nets surrounding the front door, we entered the house, removed our shoes on the dirt floor, and stepped onto the tatami (two-inch-thick straw mats). I greeted the grandfather of the family. He sat beneath a collection of antique iron teapots that hung from the ceiling. Over tea, I asked if I could return to take photographs. They consented.

On the day of my appointment with the Fujitas, the school system provided a sleek black car and a driver who spoke English. We were accompanied by the wife of the mayor and by a Japanese artist who had volunteered to assist me. Before this entourage of supporters, I set up my four-by-five-inch view camera to take my first image of tools in the barn. Japanese are accustomed to working in the middle of a crowd, but I felt inhibited. After I exposed my first sheet of film, each person peered through the camera at the upside-down image on the ground glass.

The Fujitas were unusual in their openness to me, the first *gaijin* (literally, "outside person") that they had known. As a foreigner I could not bring them the benefits that usually accrue from time-intensive relationships. But the relationship was easygoing by comparison with Japanese friendships and provided them with insight into the world beyond their somewhat isolated island nation.

The grandfather's heart condition prevented him from working on the farm, so the responsibilities had fallen to the grandmother (plate 2). Every morning she awoke before dawn to feed the animals and to begin the farm work — the transplanting or weeding — that would occupy her day. Their eldest son, his wife, and their grandchildren all lived in the same house. During the planting and harvesting seasons, the son helped with the farming, but his real occupation was demolishing old houses. His wife was in charge of the inside of the house, the cooking, cleaning, and laundry. Because of the grandfather's frail health, the stewardship of the family had passed to the fifty-year-old Mr. Fujita. He was an odd mixture of traditional rural farmer, open-minded gregarious host, and avid antique collector (plate 36). His traditional nature was clearest in his relationship with his wife. She never ate lunch with the rest of us when her husband was present. Instead she scurried between the kitchen and the dining room, providing us with delicious food.

Yet Mr. Fujita was extraordinarily accommodating to me. On my third day on the farm, he showed me the family's antique collection that he had acquired in connection with his work. Before a house was torn down and its contents discarded, he met with the owners and bought anything of value that they would sell. His antiques were stored in a concrete-block building that was almost as large as the family's main house. Once, he had rescued two elegant wooden doors from a wealthy man's home. Subsequently, he designed and built a storage building to fit around them. Although there were some rare antiques, his collection also included objects that had only sentimental value. The photographic possibilities were endless. Over time, Mr. Fujita developed a remarkable insight into my taste in subject matter. As we drove to appointments at neighbors' homes, he might point to a house, saying, "That family has a photogenic grandfather with a white beard," or "At the top of that hill is a beautiful shrine that hasn't changed since I was a child."

On cloudy days, which are so common in Japan, my chances of taking good photographs were dramatically reduced. On one such day, sensing my discouragement, Mr. Fujita decided to show me something at the top of the steep hill near his house. "Zen wa isoge" ("Do good things quickly"), he said, beckoning to me as I chased up the hill after him. As we approached a sixty-foot-long thatched-roof house at the top of the hill, I was attracted by an object in the barn and asked if I could photograph it. Mr. Fujita was adamantly opposed. This was a private, traditional family, and if we did not follow protocol I would be unwelcome and he would lose face.

At the front door he pushed open the sliding wooden door and called out, "O-jama shimasu" ("I'm sorry to bother you").

A few minutes later, the eighty-year-old grandmother poked her head through the open crack in the door. She was polite, but not friendly. Mr. Fujita asked if we might step into their entryway. It was a strange request, but he wanted to show this foreigner their dirt floor.

When we entered, he exclaimed that this bumpy earthen floor was the best in the whole valley; this family's ancestors had walked on it with *geta* (wooden platform clogs). Wasn't it exceptional? I agreed it was wonderful. He suggested we come back on my winter trip when in mid-morning the angle of light would be just right for a photograph. On our way home, he reminisced that when he was a child, just after the New Year celebrations the neighborhood children got together to watch black and white movies. They had gathered in that house, the largest in the area.

On my winter visit, phone calls were made and gifts exchanged with the neighbors; it was agreed I could photograph the floor. At the appointed time, the sun rose above the mountain behind the house as if it were under Mr. Fujita's control. Just enough light spilled into the entryway to backlight the bumpy surface (plate 1).

A friend escorted me to the winter festival of Hadaka Mairi. As a native of Morioka, the capital city in Iwate-ken, he had seen this festival each winter while he was growing up.

"If preconceived beliefs are extinguished, even a fire is cool." (Shintō o mekkyaku sureba, hi mo mata suzushii.)

When we arrived at the local shrine, people were burning their straw New Year's decorations to complete the purification rites that mark the year's beginning. Inside the gates of the shrine, grandparents pushed their grandchildren toward the front of the crowd, bowing, clapping, and throwing coins into an offering box. Parents stood in line to buy slips of paper predicting good fortune or bad in the next year.

The celebration was late in starting. Despite my down coat, sweater, wool pants, and long underwear, I was cold. By evening the sun was gone and the wind had come up; I tugged my hat over my ears to wait. Everyone left the shrine and lined the streets. The adults purchased hot, milky sake. Parents bought their children *oden* (vegetables in a hot fish-stock broth), *o-dango* (sweetened sticky rice balls), and cotton candy.

Finally, at the far end of the main street of town, a policeman signaled that the procession had begun. No one was allowed to cross the street during the next hour, for that would interfere with the purification ritual. It would be another twenty minutes before the worshipers reached us.

Parade of
Hadaka Mairi,
Iwate-ken

The crowd was suddenly quiet as the first man passed slowly before us wearing a white loincloth, a straw skirt, and a rope wrapped around his waist. After emerging from the community bath fifteen blocks away, he marched dramatically toward the shrine in the frigid winter wind. The white tracings of his breath drifted behind him in the dark street. With his left arm, he balanced a fifteen-foot bamboo pole over his head. As he stepped onto his right foot, he whisked the tip of the pole down toward the ground, causing the white ceremonial papers to flutter. Then, in a swift sweeping movement, it was erect again. As he took the balancing step with his left foot, he rang a bell in his right hand. The next man walked twenty feet behind him. With intense concentration, he too swung his pole to the earth; then, with precision, he hoisted it up and rang a bell. The procession of more than a hundred men passed before us on their slow, reverent march to the shrine where the priests were waiting. There in a private ceremony they would gather in a large tatami hall, kneeling to receive a blessing. After the religious rites were over, they would enjoy the camaraderie of a communal hot bath and would drink sake into the night.

"Did anyone ever die of pneumonia after this?" I asked my friend.

No, not that he could remember. "Shintō o mekkyaku sureba, hi mo mata suzushii" ("If preconceived beliefs are extinguished, even a fire is cool").

*I*n the winter of 1988, to find snow, I traveled to Yamagata, a prefecture on the northwest coast of the main island of Honshu. Because it is mountainous and close to the Japan Sea, Yamagata is famous for its snowy winters. But during the warm winter of 1988, instead of snow there was rain, and everything was wet and gray.

Training one's spirit.
(Seishin shūyō.)

On one dreary day, I visited a museum and saw photographs of local farmers in the village of Kurokawa acting in noh, an ancient form of Japanese theater. Until a century ago many rural communities performed these plays, but as Japan modernized, other forms of entertainment became available and noh plays became less popular. Kurokawa is one of the few rural communities where the tradition has endured; here the common people have staged the plays annually for five hundred years.

My hosts arranged for me to visit Kurokawa the following day. While I slept that night, snow fell — a wet snow of four inches. In the morning, the sun came out and intense light poured into the kitchen.

"Lucky, lucky," my friends insisted, and I agreed.

As we drove to the village, everything seemed suddenly clean; even the interior of the car was bathed in brilliant, reflected light. I noticed the weblike shadows surrounding a grove of persimmon trees and consciously restrained myself from asking to stop. Japanese friends tease me about being born in the year of the *inoshishi* (wild boar). Boars, they say, charge across roads or through fields without looking left or right, without thinking of the consequences of their actions. In Japan, there is a clear way of doing things, a definite protocol to introductions. We had an important appointment at the Board of Education and could not be late.

In a large room, fifty people sat at gray metal desks busily conducting school board business. While we waited half an hour for an information officer to be free, I sat in a padded chair and watched the snow disappearing from the pavement in the parking lot. After we met the information officer, since I am a photographer, he showed me some of the publications and calendars published on Kurokawa noh, and there were many. He brought out the most recent calendar and went through it page by page before offering it to me as a gift. When he was finished, we all bowed. I expressed my gratitude for his gracious help at such a busy time in his schedule. As we walked toward the door, I breathed a sigh of relief.

But my friend felt yet another introduction was necessary. In a separate wing of this gray building, whose interior is forever embedded in my memory, was the mayor's office. It was crucial to meet the mayor; he was a very good man. So my friend handed the secretary his business card and asked if we could see the mayor for a short visit. Yes, she would certainly make the request, but the mayor was in a meeting. So we waited.

An American expert on the Japanese had once explained to me that in Japan having a proper introduction was like swimming downstream, being pushed along by the current. Having no introduction, or a lowly introduction, was like trying to swim up a waterfall.

Indeed the mayor was a wonderful man. He was 65, short and plump, and he looked at me directly with warmth in his eyes. What had attracted me to Kurokawa? Wasn't it interesting how many foreigners came to visit this tiny village? As a child he had studied noh himself. "Seishin shūyō" ("It was a training of the spirit").

Would I like to see the rehearsal of the three-year-old boy who would make his debut this year? He would have his secretary call. What else did I want to see? Noh masks? The best noh masks were in the noh museum, but they were behind glass and no one was allowed to touch them. Occasionally the masks were aired, but photographs were particularly difficult to arrange.

As the discussion went on, I tired of asking my friend to translate the many technical words that I could not understand. The mayor's office had an excellent ground-level view of a garden; I observed that the long shadows of early morning were now short, and that the caps of snow on the dome-shaped evergreens had almost disappeared. While the mayor took a call, my friend and I were able to talk without being overheard. Yes, I agreed, he is a wonderful man, but a day like this is so rare that it must not be wasted. Tomorrow the light would be different, the snow might be gone. I must use such a beautiful day as wisely as possible.

My friend was used to balancing between what is proper and what is acceptable though slightly improper. When the mayor hung up the phone, my friend explained that I was admiring his beautiful garden and watching the light; I was eager to begin my photography. We were grateful for how generous he had been with his time, and we deeply appreciated his suggestions. I repeated some of the humble phrases I had learned and apologized for interrupting him without an appointment. It was indeed a pleasure to meet someone who protected the spirit of noh. Bowing, we left the mayor's office, and I rushed to the car. The driver drove up the mountain to show me an overview of the village while I put on my twenty-five-pound pack, which contained film, two cameras, and six lenses. When he stopped, I sprang from the car and began to work.

The following day, I attended a tofu roast. In a week, the village would be serving breakfast to the hundreds of guests who would come to the thirty-six-hour noh celebration. Roasted tofu, a traditional food, would be the main course.

The villagers had constructed a special hut using corrugated tin to safeguard a huge fire. Fifty neighbors at a time crammed into the unstable structure. To prevent the heat of the fire from searing their bare skin, they wrapped their faces with white scarves or held up cardboard with small cutouts for the eyes. The men drank cup after cup of sake. Tofu, impaled on sticks, encircled the fire. Keeping it from burning took much concentration. As I entered the hut, one of the women handed me a piece of cardboard to protect my face. When I took out my tripod, the people on either side of me knelt closer to their neighbors so I would have a place to sit.

Pointing with a long, arching stick, a woman near me shouted at a man across the circle of coals, "Turn that one, hurry. No, no, you're turning the wrong one; the next one, stupid!" The middle-aged man she was addressing moved too quickly and toppled over in drunkenness. Friends on either side helped him back to an erect sitting position and passed the sake jug around the circle once again.

Tofu Roast,
Yamagata-ken

One man jokingly pointed at my face. "Still too white," he shouted, "bake that one more."

Around noon, a group of five women left the hut and disappeared into a small barn. When they emerged, some carried umbrellas, others wore hooded straw raincoats, which would protect them from the wet snow as they walked home. I had admired the quaint shapes of straw raincoats in woodblock prints, but I had never before seen one in use.

Slipping into the barn, I quickly changed my film. Then, searching for the women, I ran down the driveway, around a corner, and down a slight hill. There in the distance, the women were walking, one behind the other, on a path between two rice fields. I chased after them, my camera pack bouncing up and down.

With great excitement, I tried to explain what a special photograph I thought they would make — the shapes of the raincoats were wonderful. Would they mind if I took their pictures? My question was followed by a pause. Finally the most outgoing woman volunteered that none of them had ever met a foreigner who spoke Japanese.

Would they mind if I took a *kinen shashin* (a remembrance photograph)? I would send them prints. Complying, the women lined up in two rows, their nervousness obvious in their stern expressions. Even when I asked

Women in Snow,
Yamagata-ken

for a smile, the tenseness remained. When I was finished, one of the grandmothers invited me to come under her umbrella so I could write down her address without getting wet.

As we crowded together with snow brushing our faces, they wanted to know what I was doing in their village and how my photographs would be used. As we became more comfortable, I asked a few of the women wearing raincoats if they would mind posing for me. Such an odd request, standing in a fixed position for a foreigner in the middle of the rice fields with the snow pouring from the sky, but they agreed (plate 56). When I felt I had imposed as long as I could, I thanked the women, who headed home, walking single file between the rice fields, giggling with pleasure.

That evening, as a result of the mayor's introduction, I was invited to the home of the noh master to see the children's noh practice. For a month and a half in advance of the performance, the all-boy cast of young actors met each evening at seven in the home of the noh teacher. When they had finished, the adult actors would come after work and practice into the night.

When I arrived, seven boys were sitting around a *kotatsu*, a low, four-foot-square table with a heater underneath. Large puffy blankets draped over the edge and formed an apron, so their legs were warm while they read comic books and watched TV. A chubby twelve-year-old boy wearing a sweatshirt was the grandson of the noh master. A slim boy of nine was the great-grandson of one of the leading noh actors in the village. The youngest child, a boy of four, had made his noh debut the previous year. His eyes were wide. Was it fatigue or wonder?

When each boy entered the room used for practice, he changed dramatically. The noh master turned on a tape of music, and the boy assumed the noh pose. Lifting his arms from his sides, he extended them forward at an angle not quite parallel to the floor. He pointed the index finger on each hand; the thumb held the other three fingers curled in his palm. One boy had an itchy nose, another wiggled during the quiet parts. During the forty-five minutes it took to rehearse each play, it was clear whether a child had a gracefulness and an ability to concentrate.

The nine-year-old great-grandson of the noh actor was a lithe boy who

Three-year-old
with Noh Master,
Yamagata-ken

had amazing poise. His part was long and intricate, involving complex work with a fan and difficult dancelike steps. He whirled and stopped, stamped his feet, moved backward, opened a fan, and waved it once before collapsing it. He whirled and stamped his feet again, changing direction. While chanting several lines of noh in a high-pitched voice, he stamped once more. Since the words used in noh are an ancient form of Japanese, I had no idea what he was saying.

On February 1, at six o'clock in the evening, the performance began as it had for hundreds of years. The villagers and visitors brought their *o-*

nigiri (rice-ball lunches), their *mikan* (tangerines), and bottles of sake; they were prepared to stay up all night crowded together on the tatami around the stage that had been set up in one of the villager's homes.

According to tradition, the three-year-old great-grandson of the host family opened the noh plays. The noh teacher carried the child to the center of the wooden stage as he might carry a valuable tea ceremony bowl. The noh teacher's left arm supported his buttocks and his right arm was wrapped around his waist. The gold and silver threads in the ancient silk kimono shone in the candlelight. Everyone became quiet. Would this child succeed? Would he remember what to say, where to stamp his foot, when to whirl?

The child walked slowly forward, heel-toe, heel-toe, one foot at a time, with his arms extended in front of him, his index fingers pointed. At the sound of the drums and the flutes, he began reciting his part in a high-pitched voice. Soon the chorus joined in with a chanting drone. The boy whirled and stamped his feet in rhythm with the drums, flipping up the long sleeve of his kimono before stamping his feet again. For fifteen minutes he charmed the audience. At last the performance was over. The boy stood still, and everyone was quiet until the noh teacher picked him up and carried him off. The boy smiled, relieved; the crowd clapped loudly.

The old people of the village say it is a mystery how such a young child remembers everything. Year after year it is always the same: the child remembers, and then after the performance, he forgets. It is one of the wonders of noh, a blessing of the *kamisama* (gods) that human beings cannot understand.

One of the boys I had seen in practice was scheduled to perform at about midnight. But instead, a girl appeared onstage in a gorgeous blue patterned silk kimono. Her long black hair was tied with a headband across the center of her forehead. A lovely halolike gold ornament shook in a coquettish way each time she moved. Her walk had exceptional grace, and as she whirled and stamped, I was captivated by her performance and amazed that such a young child could use a fan so beautifully. A woman sitting next to me explained that she was playing the spirit of a plum tree.

Female Entrance,
Yamagata-ken

In the middle of one of her twirls, she lost her place. Her father, who was singing in the chorus, called urgently in a low voice, "Backwards, whirl, stamp your foot." The noh teacher came forward and guided her in the correct direction. The child had forgotten to toss her silk sleeve over her arm as she changed direction, so the teacher placed the sleeve into the proper position. The play continued for half an hour as other characters joined the girl. I finally realized this was the boy whom I had seen practicing — girls never act in noh plays — but there was no indication of masculinity. The transformation was complete. Finally, with dramatic gestures, each character left the stage. The girl was one of the last to exit, walking in the slow, deliberate manner she had practiced. The chorus sang a final chant to the mournful sounds of the musicians. When the play was over, the crowd clapped loudly. The plays were good this year.

The noh plays continued into the night. Short comedies (kyōgen) broke the serious mood created by the noh plays to lighten the effect of the evening. Every three hours there was an intermission. The crowd spread out their o-nigiri lunches, and musicians threw tangerines into the crowd. I recognized the boy who had performed at midnight. He was now dressed in a sweatshirt and baggy pants, and he leapt playfully behind the singers. He greeted his father and then disappeared into the audience.

*T*wice a year my friend returns to her hometown, a tiny coastal town on the island of Shikoku, to visit her aging mother. At her mother's house, we knelt around the *kotatsu* (heated table), our legs covered with blankets, while her mother brought in plate after plate of delicious food.

"They fought like a dog and a monkey." (Ken en no naka.)

"O-somatsu na mono de gozaimasu ga" ("Please excuse the poor fare"), she said, bowing. While her mother was in the kitchen, I asked my friend about her mother's modesty. The food was delicious, and I hated to criticize, but at times the Japanese habit of apologizing seemed insincere.

No one takes this talk literally, she answered. "When we give a gift, we apologize for giving such a worthless present. When someone compliments us, we must deny our accomplishments or we will seem conceited. It's good manners, just part of being polite."

After dinner, I asked her mother about her childhood. For two hours she talked about some of her earliest memories. As a child, she had lived in a large house surrounded by tall trees. Each morning, she ate breakfast with her parents and brothers looking out at a rock garden. Her father was the pampered only son of a wealthy man and had no practical skills. Her family had once owned all the rice fields surrounding her ancestral home, but gradually their property had dwindled as her father sold it to pay off bad debts. He spent his life working at a low-paying office job and drinking sake in the evenings.

When she was fifteen, she and her family moved to a tiny house because the large house was taken over by creditors. She desperately wanted to go to college, but her father felt it was an extravagance for a girl. They argued over his decision, and she refused to speak to him for several weeks. But at last she acquiesced and worked to put her brothers through college by sewing kimonos. When she was twenty, her father died of a stroke.

For a woman of her era, my friend's mother had married late — when she was twenty-five. It was bad enough to be born into a family that was sliding toward disaster, but she had another black mark against her. She was born in 1906, the year of the Hinoe Uma (Fire Horse). Did I know of this legend? Certainly I knew of the twelve-year cycle of animals? All people born in a given year are supposed to have characteristics in common. Once in sixty years, every fifth cycle, women born in the year of the horse are considered to carry a curse.

It is believed that girls born in the year of the Hinoe Uma will cause their husbands to die young, so no one wants to marry them. Several centuries ago a woman born in the year of Hinoe Uma had been forced to marry someone she did not like. In her grief, she set fire to her husband's ancestral home; the fire spread rapidly in Tokyo, and much of the city burned. Many people died, including her young husband. Because of that superstition, in 1966, the most recent year of the Hinoe Uma, the birthrate in Japan dropped by almost twenty-five percent.

When her mother's marriage was finally arranged, it was to a good man who was widowed. With his three children, they moved to Kobe. But during the war, because of the bombing raids, they returned to this little village, her husband's boyhood home, and set up a small clothing shop in his mother's house; she sewed men's clothing and her husband operated the store.

The thing she hated most about moving was living with her mother-in-law, a woman born in the year of the Five Tigers, the only year with a reputation that rivals Hinoe Uma's. During the next four years they struggled with each other, showing little on the surface, but she felt "ashi o hipparu" (her legs being pulled out of their sockets). Her mother-in-law blamed her when the white radishes grew crooked and when her vegetables fetched too low a price at the local market. "Ken en no naka," my friend explained — they fought like a dog and a monkey.

During the war, her eyes became infected and her mother-in-law refused to let her go to the capital city, Tokushima, for treatment. But she rebelled and went anyway or she would now be blind. Sensing the hostility between them, her husband felt powerless. He could not choose his wife over his mother, for then he would be a disloyal son. Feeling she could bear no more, she took her two youngest daughters by the hands — one was five, the other two — and walked to the end of the wooden pier that stretched into the Pacific. She had planned to jump into the ocean with the two girls to end her misery, but at the end of the dock, she changed her mind. She would continue to endure and patiently wait to see what fate would bring.

In 1945, a tidal wave hit the village in the middle of the night. Their home was suddenly flooded. In soggy clothes, everyone rushed into the hills behind the village to keep from being carried out to sea. That night her mother-in-law caught pneumonia, and she died three days later. It was embarrassing to admit, but when this burden fell from her shoulders, it was a great relief.

*I*n Tanohata, a coastal town in northern Honshu, the afternoon air in early spring has a languid quality. An occasional fisherman and his wife sit along the wharf mending nets that stretch between them. Men walk past in rubber boots and leggings, squeaking with each step.

"Eels are not always under the willow." (Yanagi no shita ni itsumo dojō wa oranu.)

My host had made a mid-afternoon appointment for me to accompany three boats of local fishermen into the Pacific to watch them pull up their nets. The boats were two and a half hours late in returning from their morning catch; no one knew why. Finally, on the horizon, they came into view. One seemed to be tilted off center. As it drew near the dock, we noticed a twenty-foot-long bleeding shark strapped to its side.

As the men unloaded the morning's catch, the water near shore became red with the shark's blood. To my eye, the shark seemed to be breathing ever so slightly, or was it the movement of the surf? The men described finding the shark in their nets. To save the rest of the catch, they had stunned the shark, captured it, and tied it to the side of the boat. The men sawed the shark into two sections. With a pulley they loaded the tail section into the back of a pickup truck to be sold at the local market. The front half remained strapped to the boat. A few of the men hauled it out to sea and dumped it before returning to port to pick up the rest of the crew. At last the procession of three boats was ready to pull in the net for the second time that day; we were invited to board.

It took us half an hour to reach the net marked by Styrofoam balls in the open water. At positions two hundred feet apart on three sides of a triangle, the forty men hauled the net out of the water with giant pulleys, gradually pulling the boats together. In the center, the fish flailed wildly. Using hooks, the men dragged the large fish onto the deck, clubbing them into unconsciousness. With small, hand-held nets, they scooped up the little fish and dumped them into the hold of the ship. The catch was large and included valuable fish — tuna and salmon — an unexpected bonus so early in the spring.

On the way back to port, I introduced myself to a gregarious fifty-year-old fisherman and asked about fishermen's superstitions. Indeed there were some strange beliefs in the old days. Every serious fisherman had a list of "Thou Shalt Not's" tacked beside the front door of his house. Infractions brought serious consequences. Whistling was not allowed on-board, an action that was sure to bring a storm. Women were never per-mitted on fishing vessels — the *kamisama* (gods) of the ocean are women, and it was commonly thought they would resent the presence of another woman. Fishermen were forbidden to eat the meat of four-legged ani-mals. There was no point in fishing when a southern wind was blowing, for no one would catch anything.

I asked if he believed in any of them.

"No," he stated, "not in the superstitions. But there is a proverb that makes a lot of sense: 'Yanagi no shita ni itsumo dojō wa oranu'" ("Eels are not always under the willow").

"What does it mean?" I asked.

"Well, literally it means that you can't keep going back to the same place and expect to find eels, but it's used whenever someone is inflexible and keeps doing the same thing over and over again."

I asked about the shark I had seen earlier. "Was the shark still alive when you brought it into port?"

"Yes, of course," he answered.

"Why didn't you kill it before you brought it in?"

"It's not so easy to kill a shark. We had to think of the other fish in the net and protect them as best we could."

"But it seemed so sad to see it gasping near the dock."

"Saa," he said, "we don't think much about the feelings of fish in this business."

"One meeting, one chance."
(Ichi go, ichi e.)

My seventy-year-old widowed friend, Itoga Sensei, lives with her ailing mother-in-law. Until four years ago, she was an active career woman, but now she rarely leaves home. Since traditional Japanese families do not hire outsiders to nurse sick relatives, she alone cares for her mother-in-law.

On my spring trip, a mutual friend accompanied me to her home. When we arrived, we joined the ninety-three-year-old *o-bāsan* (grandmother) around a square lacquer table in the main room of the house. Despite her age, the grandmother's color was good and she was mentally alert. She bowed deeply when she saw us.

The day was warm and the sliding doors to the garden were open. The air hummed with the voices of tiny frogs that breed in the water of rice fields. Itoga Sensei asked us if we would enjoy *o-matcha* (the tea ceremony). While we talked, she offered us beancake sweets on small lacquer plates. The sweetness would create an excellent balance for the bitterness of the tea.

I was curious about her life as a young woman and asked about the postwar period. In response to my questions, Itoga Sensei shared a memory from her younger days. In those days there was never enough to eat even in rural areas, and she had a houseful of children to feed. One evening a neighboring farmer brought over a tiny pig, the runt of a large litter. The baby pig was near death, and the farmer didn't have time to take care of it. If she was willing to feed it, he would give it to her. She still remembered covering it with a blanket and slipping a baby bottle into its mouth as if it were a child. Of course it was improper to keep a pig in the house, so she built a small pen for it and fed it with whatever she could find. In time it became bigger than its brothers and sisters; her children loved it. The pig let them ride on its back and slide off its rear end. She even built a wagon, and the pig took the children for rides.

None of her neighbors had cars, and she did her errands by either walking into town or taking a bus. It was inconvenient, and she envied her friends who had bicycles. When the farmer offered to sell her pig, she accepted. The money she would receive would allow her to purchase a bicycle. She remembered seeing her pig for the last time and feeling too ashamed to look into its eyes. More than forty years had passed and she still regretted her decision.

She poured some hot water into a pottery bowl that she would use in the tea ceremony. In addition to cleaning the bowl, the water would warm the bowl so the tea would stay hot. Emptying it, she then added two scoops of green tea powder and a precise amount of hot water. Using a bamboo whisk (plate 49), she whipped the tea in a clockwise direction for a full minute and offered the first bowl to the grandmother. Itoga Sensei meticulously prepared my tea in the same manner and offered it to me with a bow. The soft green of the tea in the rust-colored bowl was exquisite. I drank it in three swallows, holding my left hand under the bowl and my right hand on the side.

"It is an exceptional bowl. What is its history?" I asked.

Someone had given it to her deceased husband twenty-five years ago. It was made by a famous potter in Shigaraki who never used glazes. She explained that the flecks of color on the bowl were caused by wood ashes falling on its surface while it was firing in a mountain kiln.

To get a better look, I lifted the bowl up to eye level, holding it in my left palm. In the meantime, Itoga Sensei whisked the tea in the final bowl for our mutual friend.

Just as we finished our tea, our conversation was interrupted by a sudden shrillness in the chirping of the frogs. "They are crying because it is about to rain," she said. As if by signal, a downpour began. Itoga Sensei rose from the table to see how hard the rain was falling. The blossoms on her three large cherry trees were almost open. In a few days she would be having an *o-hanami* (a flower-viewing party). If it rained too much, the blossoms, under the weight of the droplets, would drop to the ground, leaving nothing but fallen petals. Her guests would be disappointed.

When she came back to the table, Itoga Sensei excused herself for being un-Japanese, but she felt that she could speak openly to me since I was a foreigner and she was a modern woman. She explained that the bowl appreciation must be done within an inch of the table's surface, so that if my hands slipped, the bowl would not break. It was a mistake to hold a valuable bowl in the air because it made everyone nervous, thus destroying the feeling of calm that the tea ceremony was trying to create.

I thanked her for teaching me; she had saved me from making future mistakes. I appreciated her frankness; it was one of the reasons I cherished her friendship.

She asked if I knew the proverb "Ichi go, ichi e" ("One meeting, one chance"). "It is an old proverb," she explained. "It is said to have originated with a samurai who offered the tea ceremony to a friend about four hundred years ago. They were leaving for war and did not know if they would ever see each other again.

"Our lives seem predictable compared with the lives of the ancients, yet even we cannot be certain if we will meet again. The tea ceremony trains us to focus on the uniqueness of our moments together."

I asked if she would explain the meaning of *teisai buru* (doing something for appearances' sake), a Japanese concept that I didn't fully understand.

"We older Japanese always worry what other people think," she began. "For instance, at funerals it would be easiest to invite a country priest with a black robe to tap *poku, poku,* on a country drum and chant the last rites for one's deceased relative. But instead we invite five priests from city temples. They bring fancy altars and beautiful parasols and wear shiny purple and gold robes and bring cymbals. For the *kamisama* and the dead relative, a simple ceremony is adequate, and in fact, the chants are exactly the same. But for appearances' sake, the family must have the fancy ceremony to make a good impression on the guests." During this explanation, the grandmother had dozed off.

"When we bring gifts to someone's house, even if the gift is not from a famous department store, we carry it in the bag of a famous department store, and sometimes we even rewrap it in the box of a famous department store. The person who receives it feels more valued if it is from a place of high repute.

"At country weddings, the parents still give the bride a *tansu* (chest) full of kimonos. After the wedding ceremony, the neighbors come over to see the contents of the chest. Each drawer is pulled from the chest and each kimono is unwrapped so the neighbors can evaluate the quality. It is, of course, a foolish custom because young girls never wear kimonos anymore, so thousands of dollars go to waste. Sometimes the daughter begs her mother not to do this, but the parents must give a chest full of kimonos for appearances' sake."

As we excused ourselves, the grandmother woke up. We had intruded for a long time, and we knew both of them were tired. To say good-bye, the grandmother knelt in a prostrate bow, her head on the tatami floor and her arms extended. According to Japanese custom, I bowed as deeply as the grandmother to show respect. I stretched myself into a prostrate position and inched out of the room crawling backward.

As we walked home, I asked my friend how someone as bright and active as Itoga Sensei could bear staying at home constantly. My friend explained that Japanese women were expected to care for their in-laws. What was unusual was that Itoga Sensei loved the o-bāsan as if she were her own mother. Of course the work was hard and stressful, but Itoga Sensei had much endurance. In giving her mother-in-law such good care, she had achieved an inner peace; she would be lonely when the grandmother was gone.

*T*he pace of life in Shimoda is slow. During the day minitrucks slip through the narrow streets making deliveries, but the residents of the village ride bikes or walk. There are no large factories and no famous sites in this village just a two-hour drive from Kyoto. Old

"A frog in a well does not know the ocean."
(I no naka no kawazu tai kai o shirazu.)

women with the "bent-back syndrome" wheel baby strollers through town. They stop at the fish market, the vegetable store, and the shop that sells soy beans. After chatting with the owners, they put their purchases on the seat of the stroller and hobble down the street supported by the long chrome handle.

I had originally discovered Shimoda when I accompanied a friend to purchase a blue and white checkered teapot from the local potter. On a free day I asked if we might return.

We stopped at a tiny shop that sold film, cigarettes, candy, and liquor. I bought batteries for my flash; the couple who owned the store gave us each a can of Coke as a courtesy. An old man sitting inside on a bench near the liquor bottles waited peacefully for the day to reveal itself. Perhaps he spent more of his old-age pension here than at any other store in town, so the couple did not urge him to leave.

At the bean shop, the seventy-year-old owner was having a conversation with a woman friend over the blare of a TV soap opera. She complained to her friend that her legs were ruined from kneeling all day year after year. Now they were weak because her circulation was so poor; she could barely walk. She was content to stay here watching soap operas and having her old friends visit her. If they bought beans, all the better. Glancing up, she welcomed us.

Speaking in Japanese, I inquired if I could take a picture of her bins of beans. While I set up my camera, the owner asked her friend if she thought that foreigner was a man or a woman. They looked at me obliquely to avoid staring. They agreed that I was a man.

My friend corrected them.

The owner giggled in response. "Since she is traveling alone we thought she was a man. Anyway, she has short hair. It's difficult to tell with foreigners." Something dramatic occurred in the soap opera, and the two women became reabsorbed in the TV.

For lunch my friend had prepared rice balls wrapped in seaweed from home. We ate in a quiet shrine on a hill a block from the main street.

At three-thirty, groups of elementary-school children in blue school uniforms walked down the main street on their way home. As the first group passed, one of the children pointed at me and said, "Gaijin" (outsider). All the other children in the group turned to stare, and they too shouted, "Gaijin." The next walking group approached, and then the next. Each group pointed and repeated, "Gaijin, gaijin, gaijin." During a lull, I complained to my Japanese friend about being taunted.

"I didn't hear it," she said.

"You didn't?" I asked incredulously.

"Besides, why do you hate it so?" she asked. "After all, you are a foreigner."

"But the way it is said, fingers pointed, calling out 'Gaijin, gaijin,' without embarrassment, as if I had no feelings. It infuriates me."

When the next group of children came by, they responded like the others. "Gaijin, gaijin, gaijin."

My friend called them over. "This person from America speaks Japanese. Wouldn't you like to talk to her?"

"Haro" (hello), said one boy. "Haro, haro, haro," said the others.

She suggested they shake hands and introduce themselves.

"Haro, my name Nakamura Eiichi," said the boldest boy in loud English without eye contact. As we shook hands and I started to introduce myself, he pulled his hand away quickly and ran toward home, screaming with delight as if he had just met an *oni* (ogre) and survived. Five of his friends ran after him. The three boys who remained giggled nervously. Each of them introduced himself, stumbling over the English words and shaking my hand bravely. One boy said, "Bye bye," mimicking the singsong English that closes cartoon shows for children. The boys flashed the victory sign and ran after their classmates.

Weeks later, when I finished developing my prints from Shimoda, I sent one to the store owner who had given me a soft drink. She wrote back saying she was happy that I had found so much in her small village to photograph. I had traveled in the United States and in Japan, but she was "I no naka no kawazu tai kai o shirazu" ("like a frog in a well who does not know the ocean"). Since she had seen nothing except her little village, she was delighted to learn that it had some value.

*O*n my summer trip, I knocked on the door of one of the older women who had posed in her straw raincoat in the snow. While drinking tea and eating fresh peaches, I showed her some of my photographs. Looking at them, she was reminded that the noh costumes and masks would be aired the following day. Was I interested in taking pictures? It was an annual event that took place on the first Sunday after the end of the rainy season. No foreigner had ever been invited, but she thought her son and older brother could handle the introductions. It was fortunate that I had arrived just in time; she felt it proved that fate had brought me to the village.

"Kimono sleeves touch, a fate predetermined in a former life." (Sode furiau mo, tashō no en.)

In the early morning, fifty men who were responsible for the noh plays emptied the large private storehouse where the noh props were kept. They opened the antique chests and hung the less precious costumes on clotheslines outside. Boxes containing the valuable ancient masks and silk kimonos were delivered to a team inside the house, and the kimonos were draped over thirty-foot bamboo poles balanced between the eaves.

By mid-morning, when I arrived, most of the men had finished the hectic unpacking and had gone home. The few who remained were removing masks from fabric bags and placing them in the sun to prevent mold or insects from destroying them in the coming year. My eye fixed on the seven masks in a grid pattern in the last box. Some of the expressions were outrageous — the face of a monkey with its nose wrinkled, a demon mask with vicious teeth. My host explained that the humorous masks were used in kyōgen, comedies that were sandwiched between the more serious noh plays.

Soon, the box would be empty and the image gone. Quickly I used three apologetic Japanese phrases: "Gomen nasai. Atsukamashii onegai ga arimasu, sumimasen" ("Excuse me. I have a bold request, I'm sorry"). "I know I am imposing at an inconvenient time for you, but would you allow me to take a picture of the box of masks? I'm sorry to intrude." The host bowed to me, indicating that whatever I wanted was fine. The men chat-

Airing Masks,
Yamagata-ken

ted while I set up my four-by-five-inch view camera and barely breathed during the one-minute exposure (plate 40).

I must have seriously tested the patience of the middle-aged man who helped me that morning as I made one request after another. By midday, I had completed several still-life images using antique kimonos and had rearranged a box of antique fans. Everyone had gone home; even the owner of the house was taking a midday nap.

In the middle of the afternoon, the men returned to put everything back in order. Four men repackaged the masks; a team of twenty men folded kimonos. Another group, working outside, emptied the clothes-lines, reassembled the props, and carried all the boxes into the storage building, organizing everything carefully so the costumes for the winter noh could be easily located. When they were finished, they stretched out on the tatami mats; the air became thick with leisure. For at least an hour they enjoyed each other's company, smoking and talking, savoring the accomplishments of the day.

The following day, my grandmother friend invited me to take photographs at a gateball game. *Geitobōru,* the Japanese version of croquet, is popular among retirees all over Japan. Men and women play together with a wonderful sense of camaraderie and equality; there is much joking and teasing, but competition is fierce.

When we arrived the game had already begun. In spite of the heat, the women were covered from head to toe. Most were wearing *monpe* — baggy cotton pants with blue and white patterns. Some had wrapped their faces with white cotton strips and used hand coverings to prevent tanning.

Soon the photography session took precedence over gateball. Everyone wanted a chance to model. If I needed two models, five followed me to the site I had chosen. When I asked three of the women to walk with me to a nearby shrine, all nine volunteered to help. They tucked their gateball gear and straw raincoats under their arms and took a shortcut to the shrine. As I looked up I saw a wonderful lineup — the tall and thin, the short and plump — walking through the forest at the back of the gateball field. Everyone was chatting nonstop and stepping on the heels of the person in front. Four women who wanted to model had not been chosen for any of my photographs. At the end of the session, I asked them to

Gateball Team,
Yamagata-ken

In the Forest,
Yamagata-ken

pose for a group picture. They sat stiffly on a log at the edge of the field. After placing my camera on a tripod, I asked one of the women behind me if she could make them laugh. She clowned around near me, giving a sign repeatedly with her hands. The women guffawed, stamping their feet, rocking back and forth, and slapping their knees (plate 38). The log seemed to bounce as the whole crowd of us burst into laughter.

When I was finished, the teams resumed their game and my friend and I returned to her house for tea. A serious expression came over her face as we sat down. In polite Japanese she warned me that she was about to make a brazen request. She knew my time was precious, but could I possibly send at least one print for each of the members of the gateball team? They would be happy to pay.

I answered that they had given me a gift of their time and help. As my return gift, I would send them prints.

*T*he evening meal was finished. Six of us — the grandmother of the house, her 45-year-old daughter, and her three granddaughters — knelt around the lacquer table, munching on rice crackers as we talked. The grandmother was tradition-al in every aspect, but her granddaughters wore stylish, brightly colored western clothing. None of the girls felt comfortable kneeling for long periods, so, like me, they frequently shifted positions to keep their feet from going to sleep.

"Standing and sitting she is as lovely as a peony; walking, she moves like a lily on a long stem." (Tateba shakuyaku, suwareba botan, aruku sugata wa yuri no hana.)

In a heavy dialect, the grandmother said it was educational to have me as a guest. She had been wanting to talk to a foreigner for years. She thanked me for the Kentucky bourbon I had brought from America. Would I excuse her while she poured it into two glasses for her daughter and for me? Her son-in-law could not drink because he had stomach problems and had gone to bed early.

Realizing that Japanese etiquette prohibited the grandmother from pouring her own alcohol, I filled a glass half full and offered it to her. She accepted, admitting that this would be her first taste of liquor other than sake.

Coughing with each sip, the grandmother launched into a description of her family's history. When she used words that I didn't understand, her granddaughters translated into standard Japanese.

Hers was a family of women. That fact had shaped their lives. She was the oldest of four daughters; she had given birth to three daughters. The three girls who sat before me were her eldest daughter's only children. No sons had been born to the central branch of the family in three genera-tions. Her father had been an important man in the village. She pointed to his faded photograph, the largest of the images above the family altar. After marrying, she had continued to live in this house because her hus-band had given up his own family to be adopted by hers. This room had been a noisy place when her parents were still alive, her sisters at home, and her daughters small.

Her husband had died a year after the war was over. Imagine, he had survived the war but died of tuberculosis at home. It was a shock. At the time of his death, their three daughters had not yet married. Within weeks of her husband's death, her father died as well. It was a tragedy. With no male head of the household, there was no one to do the heavy work on the farm. An uncle decided that the only way for the family to be saved was for her eighteen-year-old daughter to marry immediately. Because so many men had been killed in the war, it was difficult to arrange marriages, so he had chosen their hired man to be her husband. After all, even though his origins were humble, he was a dependable worker.

Her daughter left the room to refill the basket of rice crackers and get some tea. While she was in the kitchen, the eldest granddaughter, Hiroko, spoke with frankness. Her father was a good man, a hard worker, but her mother had given up on life since the day she was pressured into marriage. For all these years she had quietly lived one day at a time, having no dreams of her own. In Japan, land is more important than any individual. Perpetuating the family is the most crucial thing of all.

The grandmother defended her uncle's regrettable decision. He had no other choice; it couldn't be helped.

"What would happen in such a case in America?" the youngest granddaughter asked.

"Perhaps your grandmother and her daughters could have worked the farm themselves, or they might have moved to a larger city to find work," I said.

"Leaving the family home?"

"Of course. We frequently move to find work," I replied.

"Moving was not an option in a traditional village such as this," the grandmother objected. "It would have meant neglecting our obligations to our ancestors."

The two eldest granddaughters said they shared many values with *shinjinrui* — young people of the postwar generation who had rejected the feudalistic ideas of their parents and grandparents. Hiroko was twenty-five and worked as a bookkeeper at a small electronics firm in a city twenty miles away. Her forthrightness was unusual even among people her age. Her mother worried that she had not yet found a husband whom they could adopt. Hiroko hoped for a *ren'ai kekkon* (love marriage), not a *miai kekkon* (arranged marriage). But few young men wanted to be farmers anymore, and even fewer wanted to be adopted and taken into a home dominated by women in a traditional village like theirs. If a go-between arranged for her to meet someone and he didn't appeal to her, at least she would not be pressured into marriage. Her younger sisters, still in high school, did not have to worry about such matters since they were not the firstborn. Oh, well, it would work out.

Later, talking to Hiroko privately, I asked about aspects of village life that bothered her.

"It's terrible that everything I do reflects on my family. My parents are constantly embarrassed because I'm not married," she said. "If I sit in a non-Japanese way or express my opinions too loudly, it bothers my mother because she worries about what the neighbors are thinking." The demands of neighbors are bothersome. Did I know about the traditions of gifts and return gifts? Her family sends gifts in the summer (*chūgen*) and at the end of the year (*seibo*) to people who have helped the family or who have high standing in the village. If a baby is born or if anyone in the family goes to a wedding, a party, or a funeral, either a gift or cash must be given. Within a few days, a return gift (*okaeshi*) arrives that is worth about half the value of their gift. It is all so complicated and so expensive. In addition, people gossip if the gift or the return gift are inappropriate. She quoted an aphorism that describes how well-bred women act. "Tateba shakuyaku, suwareba botan, aruku sugata wa yuri no hana" ("Standing and sitting she is as lovely as a peony; walking, she moves like a lily on a long stem").

"Have you ever tried to move like a lily on a long stem?" she asked.

"No," I answered.

"When everyone wore kimonos it was easier. In modern clothes it's impossible."

During the summer, I returned to the Fujitas' for a visit. On my first morning of photography, the grandfather pulled a chair up close to me wherever I was working. I realized he wanted me to take his photograph. While I was focusing on some iron kettles hanging from the eaves in the front of the house, he moved into the image and sat down.

"A good way to die."
(Dai ōjō.)

As a gift to the Fujitas, I brought a bottle of Kentucky bourbon, which I presented to the young Mr. Fujita after lunch in the dining room. The next day in the living room, I noticed the bottle standing before the Buddhist altar. Frequently gifts are put in front of the altar as a way of sharing the enjoyment with the ancestors, but it made me smile to see it there. "Do the ancestors like bourbon?" I asked.

Grandfather Fujita,
Iwate-ken

Mr. Fujita's sense of humor showed only in his eyes. He replied that it was a distinctly foreign taste; he thought they preferred sake.

His wife invited me to visit her oldest sister and mother, who live together in her ancestral home. The road to her home follows the river valley through rice fields to a mountainous region where tobacco plants climb the foothills. When we arrived, her mother was cutting cabbagelike vegetables in the front yard. The rest of the family was working in the fields; two black cows greeted us from the entryway of the thatched-roof house. Mrs. Fujita explained that in this part of Japan, the cows live near the family. Their stalls are part of the main house, separated from the dining room by a dirt floor.

The family's main crop is tobacco. To cure it, the husband cuts the leaves and brings them down the mountain in a wheelbarrow to a temporary plastic drying tent he rebuilds each year. He loops a rope around the stalk of each tobacco leaf and hangs it to dry (plate 34).

Late in the afternoon, I joined the family in the dining room for bean-paste sweets and tea. An uncle from next door had come to join us. As we

Mrs. Fujita
and Her Mother,
Iwate-ken

ate, I could hear a cow chewing her cud and swishing flies from her back in her stall twenty feet away.

When we returned home, the young Mrs. Fujita asked if she could touch my hair — a request she may have been wanting to make for the entire time she had known me. She took a lock of my hair into her hand, squeezing it like one might feel a peach before buying it. Indeed, she admitted, foreign hair had a strangely soft texture.

The formality of the relationship that I had with the Fujitas began to relax that summer. Grandmother Fujita asked about the details of my own family life. It made no sense to her that my husband allowed me to leave him alone for two months and go off traveling. On a previous trip, the family had met him and asked him about this. He stated quite simply that it was a sacrifice, but he believed in my work. On later visits the grandmother shook her head with disapproval and talked about what a lucky woman I was to have such a gentle husband. How could he permit me to go off on these trips when I had not produced any children? In Japan, I would be labeled a "stone woman" and divorced.

"But many modern American career couples decide to have no children," I told her.

Didn't I want children? Outsiders did have strange beliefs!

Wasn't my husband the eldest son? ("Yes.") Didn't my husband's parents think I was selfish? ("Perhaps my father-in-law wants grandchildren, but it would be impolite to say anything to me.") Did they live with us? ("No, my father-in-law is a widower and lives four thousand kilometers away. We see him twice a year.") How terrible. We were thinking only of ourselves. How could we leave him alone? It was the duty of the eldest son to take care of his father. ("But his father has his own life in California.") As a result of western influence, young people in Japan were beginning to have such selfish ideas as well. Didn't I think I lacked human feeling? What did I call my husband's father? ("I call him by his first name.") By his first name? How disrespectful. In Japan, no daughter-in-law would be so cheeky.

On each of the last two days of my summer visit, the grandfather wore a red cotton-knit Izod shirt. In the old days, red was considered too youthful a color for people over the age of twenty to wear, but since his nephew had brought the shirt home from his honeymoon in Hawaii as *omiyage* (a souvenir gift), he would use it. In addition, he proudly wore the American-made bolo tie that I had given him. The combination seemed to give him new vigor.

Before I said good-bye to the Fujita family, I suggested we take a remembrance photo. Mr. Fujita declined. "Thanks to you," he said, "there are plenty of photographs of this family."

So we all bowed; I thanked them in formal Japanese for allowing me to impose on them for so many days. As a parting gift, the grandmother slipped a white envelope into my hand. She said I should use it to buy a gift for my husband; I had left him alone far too long to be safe. On the way into town in the back seat of the car, I opened the envelope; it contained a Japanese bill worth $80. My Japanese friend who was driving said it was a gift from the heart, not an obligatory return gift. It reflected the Fujitas' feeling that I was like a family member leaving on a long trip who might need extra money to be sustained.

I never got a photo of the grandfather in his red shirt.

A week after my departure, I received a call from the mayor of Ishidoriya, who, with difficulty, had located me in central Japan. Grandfather Fujita had died suddenly of a heart attack. He had not lingered but had passed away quietly in his own home. It was a good way to die ("Dai ōjō"). Would I mind sending a telegram to be read at the funeral?

*S*ome Japanese believe that the spirits of departed ancestors return to their ancestral homes for a three-day visit in August. The O-bon festival, a national holiday, celebrates their return. For a week, crowds of people escape from the cities; they pack themselves into trains, buses, cars, and airplanes to visit their relatives in rural areas.

"Tearful rain."
(Namida ame.)

My friend Miyuki-san invited me to spend O-bon at her childhood home on one of the islands of Gotō Rettō, an archipelago off the coast of Kyushu in southern Japan. Her parents still lived there, and she planned to visit with her children. To reach Kyushu, the five of us stood on a train for half a day supported by the bodies around us. From a southern port in Kyushu we purchased tickets for the ferry. During the three-hour ferry ride, Miyuki-san explained that her father would be so excited to see us that he might be a little overgregarious in his welcome. As I would soon see, people from her village were much less inhibited than most Japanese. Each year, for eleven months, her parents waited for their children and grandchildren to return from Tokyo, Shizuoka, and Osaka. In August, for one week, their home bulged with relatives and activity. Her father would be ecstatic to have everyone back. My visit had made them nervous, but she had tried to reassure them.

It was dark when we finally arrived. Miyuki-san's father, as well as her sister, brother, nieces, and nephews, who had all arrived earlier, waved to us from the dock. As we disembarked with two hundred other visitors, her father hugged Miyuki-san and vigorously shook hands with me. He hauled our luggage home in a cart behind his bicycle; a car was unnecessary when everything he needed was a five-minute bike ride from his house.

A feast of raw seafood awaited us. Slices of abalone, tuna, and squid circled a platter, but it was the octopus that gave everyone the most pleasure. That morning, Miyuki-san's father had found it in one of his cagelike traps. He invited his grandsons to go with him early the next morning to find more.

After dinner, one by one, thirteen of us entered the *o-furo* (hot bath), using the same water to bathe. Since Japanese soap and rinse themselves before entering the hot bath, the water was still quite clean when I took my turn after the grandchildren but before the other adults. According to Japanese etiquette, guests enter the *o-furo* first, but Miyuki-san had asked her parents to treat me like a family member. That night, six grandchildren and two adults slept on the tatami in the living room, and three adults slept in a bedroom upstairs. The grandparents laid out their futon on the tatami in a small room off the kitchen.

Miyuki-san's father and her two sons were gone when the rest of us woke up the next morning. When the sons returned they were shouting happily. Each proudly held out an octopus. The slimy legs were so intertwined with the boys' fingers that it was difficult to distinguish one from the other. The youngest boy carried his gooey prize over his head and thrust it at his mother to see if he could scare her. Miyuki-san's father smiled broadly. It was a good omen finding octopus two days in a row.

At ten o'clock a horn sounded to announce the beginning of a boat race. Everyone rushed to the wharf where five crude wooden boats waited, one for each neighborhood team. There were nine children in each boat.

Grandmothers
with Umbrellas,
Nagasaki-ken

Three pairs of kneeling children, all dressed in the same color, held their paddles expectantly. In addition, one child knelt near the center of the boat with a drum between his legs; another stood at the stern; the strongest paddler knelt at the head of the boat. At the sound of a gun, the five boats surged forward. The drummer beat out a rhythm; the standing boy yelled, "Yoisho!"("Heave ho"), and seven of the children dug their paddles into the water, pulling and feathering together.

The racecourse took the boats around two buoys half a mile away. As the boats rounded the second buoy, the grandmothers began to scream and wave their umbrellas as if their effort would cause the boats to go faster. One hundred feet from the finish, three of the boats were almost even. The crowd, on its feet, screamed encouragement. The children wearing red looked bigger and stronger, but the greens' boat slid forward to win by a foot at the finish line. The relatives of the greens cheered and praised the wet children as they docked the boat. After eating rice balls and chocolate bars, they would race two more times that afternoon.

The village men raced next, and then the women. Since there were so few young adults in the village, they could no longer fill the boats, so relatives from Tokyo and Nagoya tied the neighborhoods' colored bandannas around their heads and joined the races.

Behind Miyuki-san's parents' home, a large graveyard extended up the mountain. As twilight approached, each of the families in the village carried paper lanterns to its ancestral grave plot. The grandfathers lit candles and strung paper lanterns in rows from bamboo poles as beacons to guide the return of the ancestors. The children carried incense and firecrackers. As night fell, a thick smell of incense covered the mountain. Firecrackers exploded, banging and popping, sending sparks into the air.

"Why the firecrackers?" I asked.

"The dead would not want to return to a solemn occasion," Miyuki-san explained. "The festive atmosphere lures them home."

As she spoke, the brilliant lanterns swung in the night wind, and streaks of light ascended into the dark sky. Finally, when the children had run out of sparklers and firecrackers, they ambled home, and the grandfathers

Candlelit Lanterns,
Nagasaki-ken

blew out the candles. They collapsed the lanterns and carried everything down the mountain to be used again the next evening.

On each of the three days of O-bon, the cycle of activity was the same. On the final evening, the villagers believe that the ancestors return to the otherworld. After the lanterns were hung up and taken down for the last time, the villagers gathered at the local temple for a blessing.

At twilight we drove to Aokata, a nearby village, that is famous for its *shōrōbune* (boats with lanterns). Eight-foot boats loaded with food for the ancestors' journey were covered with festive decorations and lanterns. From the wharf, a large boat would tug them out to sea, where they would be released to drift and sink on the voyage to the otherworld.

As we gathered on the wharf, we heard rumblings of thunder. The young men rushed to lower the gift-bearing boats into the water, tying one behind another. Pulled by a large boat, the string of small boats circled the harbor three times, the lanterns glowing. On each pass, a new

Gift-Bearing
Boats,
Nagasaki-ken

round of fireworks burst into the night sky. Thirty older women stood next to us on the concrete pilings and moved prayer beads through their gnarled hands, chanting Buddhist sutras in a low and endless monotone. People who had lost relatives that year wept quietly. As the boats made their third pass, the storm broke and a downpour of rain hit the streets. An old woman next to me looked up at the sky so the rain would wash over her face. "Namida ame" ("tearful rain"), she said quietly.

*T*hrough a Buddhist priest, I learned of a seventy-year-old nun who had founded a day-care center in the hills of Shiga-ken in central Japan.

"There is discipline to emptiness."
(Mu no hataraki ari.)

It was arranged that two friends would accompany me on a visit to meet her in late August. When we arrived on a rainy afternoon, we bowed deeply. She greeted us and then faced the statue of the Hotokesama (Buddhist god) and began to chant. The priest who had introduced us handed us each a *mokugyo* (wooden drum) and a pillow for kneeling. There was a gentleness to the sound of the drum, like the croaking of a bullfrog, as five of us tapped in rhythm. Slowly the chanting drew to a close; somehow we all knew when to stop.

The nun sat in a dark corner of the large room and told the story of her life, gesticulating throughout the conversation. It was raining; the sliding paper screens were open. Outside, a hollow piece of bamboo on a pivot emptied and filled with water, tapping rhythmically.

Much later, the nun turned to me, knowing that I wanted to take a photograph. I asked her to move to the entrance of the room where the light was better. There she knelt in a still, meditative pose. But, it was the animated demeanor of this woman that had captured my interest. Would she continue with the story of her life? Completely forgetting the camera, the nun spoke with great intensity (plate 9).

At the age of five, her parents had brought her to this convent. They believed that good fortune would come to nine generations of their descendants if one of their daughters became a nun. Even though her parents were not poor, the decision was made.

It was a lonely time for her. She had to eat the "cold food given by strangers," and her family did not visit. Like all novices, her head was shaved. Because she was so young, she had to go to elementary school with regular children. Of the three hundred students in the school, only two of them had shaved heads. Because she looked strange, other students teased her and even beat her with sticks. She wonders if some brain damage resulted, because she is still terrible at math. She did well in her other subjects and was a healthy child. "Namu Amida Butsu, Namu Amida Butsu," she chanted, seeking the mercy of the Hotokesama.

During the war, as a young woman, she and another nun wandered from village to village ringing a bell and begging for food and lodging. She envied all the possessions that other people had, for they seemed to have so much and she had nothing. But when she was invited into their homes, she learned that there was some profound unhappiness in each person's life that was not evident on the surface. She chanted and chanted, seeking the mercy of the Hotokesama.

When she was mature enough to truly look inside herself, she realized in her heart that she did not have a deep belief in the Hotokesama. Her conscience bothered her, for on the surface she was a nun, but underneath she harbored such deep and painful doubts. Her skepticism persisted for years, causing her great stress. "Namu Amida Butsu, Namu Amida Butsu," she chanted, seeking the guidance of the Hotokesama.

At the age of fifty, during this period of doubt, she received a great kindness. She developed a serious illness. Over three years, she had several stomach operations and was constantly in bed. She was terribly lonely and chanted, "Namu Amida Butsu, Namu Amida Butsu," continually. For months, she felt the presence of the Hotokesama before her, as if they were meeting face to face. Her stress disappeared, and she felt at peace.

She now believes deeply in the mercy of the Hotokesama, but her illness taught her something new about this mercy. If an ox has two huge bags of rice on its back, rather than removing one, the mercy of the Hotokesama is to add another.

Chanting "Namu Amida Butsu, Namu Amida Butsu," has become as natural to her as breathing, and she feels a wonderful sense of calm. Before long, she hopes the Hotokesama will invite her to return to heaven. Patiently, she awaits the call.

*I*t is a strange concept that land, less than half an acre, could determine the form and direction of a man's life. Mr. Takeuchi was born the eldest son of a family with a deep history. He never thought to question that he would marry, live, and die in Nishidera. His oldest grandson was only thirteen, but everyone assumed that he, too, would never move.

"By inquiring into the past, one understands the present."
(Furuki o tazunete, atarashiki o shiru.)

Sixteen generations of his family had lived in the village of Nishidera (Western Temple) in Shiga-ken.

"On this very piece of land?" I asked.

"Yes, here," he answered, pointing toward the earth that lay under the foundations of the house as if I ought to be able to see the giant roots that had held him here.

"If you moved to another place, would you still be considered the sixteenth generation?"

"No, I would be the first generation on the new land, and I would be a disgrace to my family."

If one were to look at Mr. Takeuchi on a train, watch him hail a cab, or judge him by his bearing or clothing, there would be nothing to indicate that he was different from any other sixty-five-year-old. But inside his home, the home with five-hundred-year-old roots, the difference was obvious. The thatched house itself wasn't so old, only about three hundred years, but the garden had been laid out five hundred years ago. The first ancestor who had moved here had selected and positioned these rocks with the aid of a gardener. Once placed, no one had moved them. Everything else was built around them. It was not an elaborate garden that simulated the edge of the sea or the top of a mountain. It was humble, yet he imagined he understood his ancestor's thoughts by looking at the placement and choice of the few rocks and trees.

In the corner near the house his ancestors had carved a basin in a stone centuries ago. While washing his hands in this ancient hollow he knew he was viewing the garden from one of the locations his ancestors had intended. The black pine in the corner might be as old as the garden, although he couldn't be sure, for, in any garden, the trees change. He pointed to the *momiji* (Japanese maple) that dominated one section of the garden with its extended branches. I was seeing this tree in its best season — the fall — when the leaves turn a brilliant red before dropping on the moss. Years ago, an ancestor had roped down its lower branches so it would have an elegance for the descendants of this house.

Mr. Takeuchi's ancestors were originally from Kyoto; they were probably forced to move here by the shogunate. At that time, few Japanese could read or write, and since his ancestors were literate, they were sent to act as the link between this village and the ruler of the area. Did I know that his family had been the repository of all the temple records over the years? The old manuscripts were in the next room on the shelf if I wanted to see them. He excused himself and returned carrying an expandable folder. Out of it he pulled a stack of documents and two scrolls. He placed them carefully on a low table.

His oldest document had been dated at 1289, precisely seven hundred years before. I stared with disbelief at the sheet of rice paper. The text was short, and it read from top to bottom and right to left. A professor of ancient Japanese had translated it, but even the translation was difficult to read. It contained complex kanji (Chinese characters) that Mr. Takeuchi didn't know; he stumbled as he tried to read. "It is said ancient Buddhist texts are buried under the mound on the hill. Do not cut the trees on the mound."

Next, Mr. Takeuchi opened a tattered 350-year-old scroll that related to the suppression of Christians. Insects had nibbled on much of the scroll, leaving worm-shaped holes that threatened to enlarge as he unwound it. Years ago a fresh piece of *washi* (handmade paper) had been attached to the back by a Kyoto scroll expert, but the insect damage had persisted. The entire scroll was about seven feet long. He insisted on unrolling every inch. "The document forbids people in this village from believing in Christianity," he stated, paging through a reference book to find a translation.

As the village scribe, Mr. Takeuchi's ancestor had written the names of the villagers who were present at the time this document was first read. The head of each household had pressed an o-shaped stamp next to his name to signify he would obey this edict.

"Are the descendants of these families still living in the village?" I asked.

A few had moved away and a few had come in, but the population of the village had remained stable at fifty *ken* (households) or about two hundred people. In his own case, an extra Takeuchi family moved here 550 years ago. His ancestor's younger brother had purchased property on the other side of the temple. Two or three new families had moved into the area in the last few years, but they lived on the outskirts of town.

Occasionally the villagers were *urusai* (bothersome) about the proper way of doing things. The thing he disliked the most was catching neighbors looking through the fence, trying to see who was coming and going. But he had no choice but to live here and follow the ways of the village.

In some ways it made his life very simple to have so many things predetermined. It was as easy as riding a train to Kyoto.

But at times it was difficult. To keep from embarrassing the good name of his ancestors, he had to live a careful life. As the oldest son and heir of his family, he still bore the five-hundred-year-old duty of village scribe. Soon many of the older generation would die; during the next several years he would photograph them and record their histories. It was a time-consuming task, but he enjoyed the responsibility. It was not the sort of work that broke your bones and offered only fatigue as a reward.

Mrs. Takeuchi entered with hot water, tea bowls, and sweets. Behind her was their ten-year-old grandson wearing a Mickey Mouse sweatshirt. He wanted to join us rather than watch the Sunday cartoons on television. She closed the sliding door with difficulty. Mr. Takeuchi said it was inconvenient living in such an old house; the warping doors were just one of many problems. But in the big modern houses, it was hard to get one's soul to feel at ease. He had no plans to modernize.

Mrs. Takeuchi was preparing to serve *matcha.* She began by tapping the powdered tea into a pottery bowl. While she was adding hot water, her grandson asked if he could help. The boy gracefully whipped the tea into a froth and handed the first bowl to me. His grandmother praised his mixing technique but said that when he offered the bowl to a guest he must use two hands, not one. He should also bow ever so slightly. This could only be achieved if he knelt instead of sitting cross-legged. The boy was up for the challenge. When he served his grandfather, everything was right. The grandparents beamed. After preparing a bowl of tea for his grandmother and himself, he grabbed a handful of pretzels dipped in chocolate from the center of the table and ate them, getting chocolate on his hands. After drinking his tea, he lay down on the tatami next to his grandfather to read an inch-thick comic book.

When I arrived at the Fujitas' for a visit on a cold morning in mid-January, Mr. Fujita and his demolition crew were drinking tea and warming their hands around a wood-burning stove near the entrance. We bowed and exchanged the formal greeting of the New Year. As soon as I had removed my shoes and stepped onto the tatami mats, the grandmother seized my hand, saying we must call grandfather. He always enjoyed my visits and would want to know that I was back. She led me to the *butsudan,* a large open cupboard set into the wall of the living room where the ancestors are honored. Hung in a line just above the butsudan were drawings and photographs of deceased relatives. In the center of the row among the other images, a familiar face — Grandfather Fujita — stared down at me. The photograph had been added as a remembrance since my last visit.

"When one speaks of next year, the ogres laugh." (Rainen no koto o iu to oni ga warau.)

We knelt quietly side by side. Grandmother Fujita lit two candles, placing them in front of the gold-leaf altar. The brilliant interior of the cupboard glowed in the wavering reflected light. After lighting a stick of incense, she tapped a small gong three times with a tiny mallet, clapped her hands, and bowed. She then returned to the kitchen, leaving me alone.

Copying the grandmother, I tapped the gong, clapped, and bowed. As the high-pitched ring echoed around me, I felt the sting of unexpected sadness. Tears welled up in my eyes. It suddenly seemed possible that Grandfather Fujita knew that I had returned.

The following day, the Fujitas were commemorating Koshōgatsu (little New Year). New Year's, observed on the first, second, and third of January, is Japan's most important annual holiday. Koshōgatsu is celebrated in isolated rural areas where the winters are long and people have energy and free time to participate. It is an informal holiday by comparison with New Year's. On the appointed day neighbors, friends, and distant relatives gather for *mochi* making.

On the morning of the celebration, Grandmother Fujita and her daughter-in-law had gotten up early to steam the special mochi rice. Mr. Fujita brought a special log two feet in diameter out of the barn; the top had been carved in the shape of a bowl. After it was cleaned, his wife placed the first batch of hot rice in the concave top, and the mochi pounding began. Mr. Fujita lifted a large pole that would serve as the mallet and smacked it into the mochi. As he lifted the wooden shaft, his mother readjusted the rice. Just as she withdrew her hands, he brought the pole down with a resounding whack. Whenever he raised the shaft, she quickly turned over the white mass and pulled her hands out of the way. After long years of practice, they worked in perfect rhythm. Cousins, second cousins, grand-nieces and -nephews, all had come to participate in the mochi making. A boy of six tried to pound the mochi but he couldn't lift the wooden pole. The older children were out of shape and had to be relieved after a few blows.

While the mochi was still warm it was patted with rice flour and divided into flat round cakes. Some would be offered to the ancestors, some would be toasted and eaten as snacks, and some would be put into *o-zōni*, the special soup of the New Year. In the cities, people now use food

Pounding
Mochi,
Iwate-ken

Rolling
Mochi Dough,
Iwate-ken

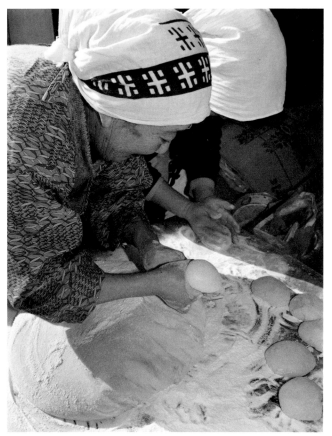

processors to make mochi, but everyone agrees that handmade mochi is vastly superior.

By noon, the mochi making was finished. Over lunch, Mr. Fujita poured sake for the adults. We toasted, wishing everyone good fortune and good health in the coming year. In lacquer bowls, his wife had poured a fish-flavored stock over a warm square of mochi to make o-zōni. With chopsticks, we tried to pinch the sticky mochi into small pieces, slurping the soup to express our pleasure. After lunch, Grandmother Fujita went from shrine to shrine in the neighborhood, offering more than fifty mochi to the *kamisama*. She hoped her respectfulness to them would be repaid with kindness to her family.

In the winter in northern Japan, it is almost dark by five o'clock. At twilight, Mr. Fujita and I were sitting in the formal dining room watching the light gradually withdraw from the rocks in the garden outside. In the *tokonoma* (an alcove in the wall) hung one of his prized possessions — a *sumie* scroll depicting Daruma (a chubby old man with a beard). I had admired it on previous visits. He had bought it when he was young, paying more for it than he could afford. Now he could sell it for many times what he had originally spent, but he had decided to keep it. Did I know the story of the Daruma? Years ago an old man seeking enlightenment sat and stared at a wall. For years he never moved. Eventually he lost the use of his arms and legs, but he continued his meditation and attained enlightenment.

He pointed to a modern Daruma in the corner of the room. The round, red heads made of papier-mâché are sold at temples at the start of the New Year, he explained. The face has especially large blank white eyes. When someone makes a wish, one of the eyes is painted black, but the second eye is blackened only if the wish comes true. Each New Year, the previous Daruma is returned to the temple and a new one is purchased. Some people make the same wish over and over again until it finally comes true. "Because a Daruma is not perfectly round, if you knock it over it will eventually right itself, since it has a weighted, flat base. We have a saying, 'Nana korobi, ya oki' ('Seven times down, eight times up'). It is a very Japanese way of thinking."

"Do you believe that you will get your wish?" I asked.

"There's no point in buying a Daruma if you don't believe it," he said.

The day of mochi making was over. As I was leaving, I expressed my appreciation to the family for the delicious mochi and thanked them for including me in such a personal celebration.

The grandmother asked when I would be coming to Japan again.

"Maybe next year," I answered. Suddenly, I remembered a proverb I'd learned from a friend. "Rainen no koto o iu to oni ga warau" ("When one speaks of next year, the ogres laugh").

It was one of Grandmother Fujita's favorite proverbs, and she was delighted that I had learned it. "Mata, irasshai," she said, inviting me back.

When the taxi arrived to take me to the train, Mr. Fujita, his wife, and his mother escorted me to the car. As I disappeared into the darkness, they bowed and waved, bowed and waved, and bowed.

My hut at New Year's,
nothing much to it.
But — everything.

(*Sodō*)

1. EARTHEN FLOOR, Iwate-ken

2. READING THE NEWSPAPER, Iwate-ken

3. KITCHEN POTS, Shiga-ken

4. SEACOAST VILLAGE, Yamagata-ken

5. PAGODA, Yamagata-ken

6. BAMBOO FOREST, Tokushima-ken

7. MELTING SNOW, Yamagata-ken

That's good,
this is also good.
Spring in my old age.
  (*Ryōto*)

8. TAMURA SENSEI, Shiga-ken

9. BUDDHIST NUN, Shiga-ken

10. TOKONOMA WITH SCROLLS, Iwate-ken

11. ANCESTORS' BOOKS, Yamagata-ken

12. GOD OF WEALTH, Shiga-ken

In the morning mist,
brush paintings.
A dream of people floating past.
  (*Buson*)

13. BAMBOO SHADOWS, Shiga-ken

14. ASUKE VILLAGE, Aichi-ken

15. TEA BUSHES, Kyoto-fu

16. PLANTING RICE, Iwate-ken

17. SPRING RAIN, Aichi-ken

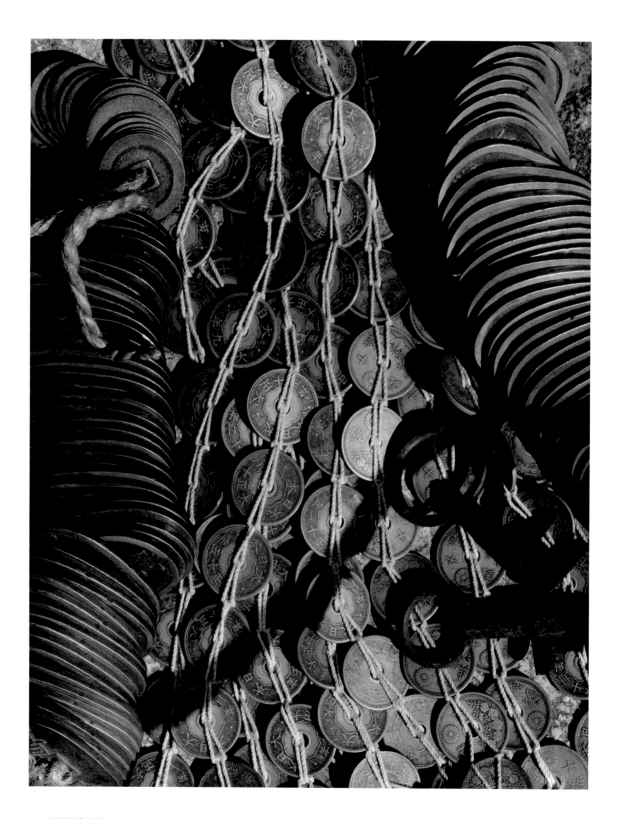

18. ANTIQUE MONEY, Iwate-ken

19. NINETEEN FISH, Shimane-ken

20. DRYING SQUID, Shimane-ken

21. FISHING WHARF, Aomori-ken

From which tree in flower
I'm not sure,
but, ah, what fragrance!

(*Bashō*)

22. MAGIC GARDEN, Aichi-ken

23. THE WAY OF THE BOW, Kanagawa-ken

24. SHINTO PRIEST, Shimane-ken

25. GIRLS' DAY DOLLS, Yamagata-ken

26. POTTER'S STUDIO, Kōchi-ken

What's that — underwater?
Vermillion carp passing —
noon's cherry blossoms.

(Sawaragi)

27. SWIMMING CARP, Shimane-ken

28. LOTUS LEAVES, Saga-ken

29. AFLOAT, Nagasaki-ken

30. TIE-DYEING, Aichi-ken

31. INDIGO DYEING VATS, Shiga-ken

Closing the umbrella,
escaping
under young leaves.
   (Shiki)

32. GRAPE VINEYARD, Yamagata-ken

33. MENDING NETS, Tokushima-ken

34. TOBACCO CROP, Iwate-ken

35. TAILOR'S WINDOW, Aichi-ken

36. MR. FUJITA AND THE DARUMA SCROLL, Iwate-ken

37. STREET VENDOR'S CART, Gifu-ken

38. GATEBALL PLAYERS, Yamagata-ken

39. SHAMISEN IN AN ATTIC, Aichi-ken

40. NOH AND KYŌGEN MASKS, Yamagata-ken

41. YOUNG VISITORS, Yamagata-ken

42. STRINGS OF PERSIMMONS, Iwate-ken

43. SORTING SOYBEANS, Iwate-ken

44. BROOMS ON A CLAY WALL, Iwate-ken

Autumn, beneath the eaves
a man sells bolts of fabric
under the drying radishes.
   (*Kyoshi*)

45. BACKLIT RADISHES, Iwate-ken

46. RICE HARVEST, Iwate-ken

47. EIGHTY-YEAR-OLD FARMER, Saga-ken

48. TEA CEREMONY KETTLES, Iwate-ken

49. BAMBOO WHISKS, Nara-Ken

50. SHIITAKE LOGS IN WINTER, Iwate-ken

51. WATAMUKI SHRINE, Shiga-ken

Sleet on the old pond.
A sandal
floats to the bottom.

(Buson)

52. POND IN WINTER, Yamagata-ken

53. EIGHT FOLLOWERS OF BUDDHA, Aomori-ken

54. TEMPLE OF CARVED STONES, Shiga-ken

55. MOUNTAIN VILLAGE, Yamagata-ken

56. WALKING HOME IN THE SNOW, Yamagata-ken

Among winter's trees
ancient, ancient
sounds.
  (*Issa*)

57. SNOW-COVERED ROOFTOP, Yamagata-ken

Notes to the Plates

1. EARTHEN FLOOR, Kamega-
mori, Ōhasama-chō, Hienuki-gun,
Iwate-ken

Until a hundred years ago, the floors
in the vestibules of most rural homes
were made of a mixture of clay and salt.
Now, most earthen floors have been replaced by concrete, which is easier to
keep clean. Guests remove their shoes or
wooden platform sandals in the entryway
before stepping on the tatami.

2. READING THE NEWSPAPER,
Kamegamori, Ōhasama-chō, Hienuki-
gun, Iwate-ken

Grandmother Fujita can kneel with
great ease, despite her age. When she
was a child, there were no chairs in her
home, so from the beginning she learned
to kneel. Because chairs and sofas are
now common in homes, many of the
younger generation have lost the ability
to kneel for long periods.

3. KITCHEN POTS, Kōsei-chō,
Shimoda-gun, Shiga-ken

This kitchen is in the ancestral
home of a family who have practiced indigo dyeing for six generations. In 1970,
the family added a modern kitchen, allowing this space to be used exclusively
in the dyeing process. Skeins of cotton
yarn are soaked in the metal pots before
they are dyed in indigo.

4. SEACOAST VILLAGE, Yura-chō,
Tsuruoka-shi, Yamagata-ken

The western coast of Japan is known
as the *ura*, or backside, of Honshu, the
main Japanese island. When storms hit
this spectacular coastline, the Sea of Japan becomes dark, and waves of ten to
twenty feet pound the shore. Coastal
towns have built extensive seawalls to

protect their homes and businesses. The middle-aged and older men of this village are fishermen, but most of the young men have left the village to become "salarymen" in the cities.

5. PAGODA, Dewa Sanzan, Haguro, Yamagata-ken

This six-hundred-year-old pagoda stands in a forest of ancient Japanese cedar. During the summer months, thousands of religious pilgrims descend into this valley, walking past the magnificent pagoda before ascending the 2,446 steps, which lead them to a group of temples and shrines called Dewa Sanzan at the top of Mount Haguro. In telling the history of the area, local monks describe the period following the Meiji Restoration when the government required the separation of Shintoism and Buddhism. Sects in which they were combined, like Dewa Sanzan, were often demolished by the reformers. Fortunately, this pagoda was left standing. It is now a national treasure.

6. BAMBOO FOREST, Awa Fukui, Anan-shi, Tokushima-ken

Bamboo forests produce *take no ko* (bamboo shoots), a delicacy eaten in the spring. Shoots emerge from the web of roots and grow to the height of about ten inches before they are cut and sent to restaurants in Kyoto and Osaka. To accelerate the growth of the shoots, the owners cut some of the bamboo so the sun can penetrate the forest and warm the base of the plants. Eventually, the fallen bamboo will be used in making household products.

7. MELTING SNOW, Ōsone, Yamagata-shi, Yamagata-ken

Rice continues to be the primary crop of many small farmers in Japan. The paddies are dormant during the winter. In the spring, the farmers plow under the old stalks and mix fertilizer into the moist soil. To make sure the paddy holds water efficiently, they pound clay into the base of the field and into the cracks in the elevated sides.

8. TAMURA SENSEI, Higashidera, Ishibe-chō, Kōga-gun, Shiga-ken

The retired director of a home for retarded children, Tamura Sensei is a published author and prolific artist. He introduced me to Japanese proverbs and folk tales in 1968 and has continued to be a source of inspiration. To show respect, the term *"sensei"* (literally, teacher) is used instead of *"san"* (Mr., Mrs., Miss) after someone's family name.

9. BUDDHIST NUN, Gamo-chō, Shiga-ken

As a practitioner of Amida Buddhism, this nun believes that through chanting she will receive assistance from the Amida Buddha. She repeats the chant "Namu Amida Butsu" thousands of times in a single week. It is a prayer as well as a form of meditation.

10. TOKONOMA WITH SCROLLS, Kamegamori, Ōhasama-chō, Hienuki-gun, Iwate-ken

The *tokonoma* — a shallow alcove in the living room — is the aesthetic focus of a traditional home. A flower arrangement, a single scroll, or valuable pottery bowls are displayed here. When guests visit, the visitor of the highest rank is seated with his back to the tokonoma.

There are several possible tokonoma designs, but rules governing the proportions and basic structure are precise and rigidly followed; only the most elegant include a window covered with *washi* (handmade paper).

11. ANCESTORS' BOOKS, Ōyama, Tsuruoka-shi, Yamagata-ken

The woman who inherited these books is uncertain which of her ancestors collected them. She assumes it was her great-grandmother, who loved kabuki (a form of Japanese theater). Her family's *kura* — a thick-walled storage house — is filled with the objects collected by nineteen generations of ancestors. Historically, kura held the most valuable of the family's possessions — family heirlooms, as well as seeds and rice for the crops of the coming year. The thick walls protected the contents from fire and insects and maintained moderate temperatures.

12. GOD OF WEALTH, Shōjuzenji, Tsuchida-chō, Ōmihachiman-shi, Shiga-ken

This deteriorating 150-year-old statue measures one meter high and is located in a Zen temple complex. Statues of the smiling Gods of Wealth (Hōtei Oshō) are common in temples throughout Japan. Offerings of flowers and fruit are placed before the god in the belief that they will bring good luck.

Since World War II, this Zen temple has declined in importance. In the late eighties the resident Zen monk died, and now a monk from another temple visits just once a month to perform rites and ceremonies.

13. BAMBOO SHADOWS, Higashidera Kōga-gun, Shiga-ken

The tiny town of Higashidera is best known for a beautiful twelve-hundred-year-old temple — a national treasure — for which the town is named. The priest and his family live in a modern dwelling near the temple. A six-foot-high stucco wall gives them privacy from the street. In late afternoon, bamboo trees growing on a hillside create shadows on the dwelling's exterior walls.

14. ASUKE VILLAGE, Asuke-chō, Higashikamo-gun, Aichi-ken

Japanese treasure the moment in spring when the *sakura* (cherry) trees are in full bloom. The flowers remain on the branches for just two or three days. In late March and early April, television stations report the percentage of cherry blossoms in bloom in different parts of the country. At the height of the season, some companies bus their employees to the local park for the day, where they eat, drink, and sing, accompanied by blaring tape recorders. They renew their commitment to the company's goals while enjoying the beauty of the swirling blossoms.

Asuke is a historical village an hour east of Nagoya. Local craftsmen demonstrate the local traditions of silk production and umbrella-making.

15. TEA BUSHES, Uji, Wakka-chō, Soraku-gun, Kyoto-fu

Uji is one of several areas in Japan famous for its tea. The tea bushes are planted on the sides of mountains so that the hot afternoon sun will not strike the leaves and make them bitter. At the beginning of May, the leaves are picked and dried. "New" tea from the current crop is considered a delicacy.

16. PLANTING RICE, Kamegamori, Ōhasama-chō, Hienuki-gun, Iwate-ken

In early spring, farmers in Iwate-ken sow grains of rice in makeshift greenhouses, carefully controlling the temperature and humidity while there is still danger of frost. In mid-May, when the rice is a foot high, it is transplanted into the flooded rice paddy. On this day in 1987, ten women worked from sunrise to dusk to transplant the rice using this centuries-old method. The following year, the Fujitas switched to a mechanized system. Two people riding on a specially designed small tractor planted this field in one day.

17. SPRING RAIN, Asuke-shi, Aichi-ken

In early April, there is a sense of renewal throughout Japan. April marks the beginning of the school year, it is the month when recent graduates are hired by companies, and it is an auspicious time to marry. In the spring there is only occasional rain in this region. It isn't until June that the rainy season, *tsuyu*, arrives.

18. ANTIQUE MONEY, Kamegamori, Ōhasama-chō, Hienuki-gun, Iwate-ken

Collecting coins has been a passion of Mr. Fujita's since he was eight years old. His mother describes how at a young age, he saved to buy antique coins rather than spending his extra yen on sweets. The large oblong coins on the right and left are approximately two

hundred years old; the round coins, minted in the twenties, are more common. The holes in the center, created during the casting process, provided an easy way to carry coins on a strand of rope.

19. NINETEEN FISH, Okidomari, Yatsuka-gun, Shimane-ken

These black sea bream (*kurotai*) are fresh off the boat. One of the fishermen threw them into this Styrofoam box as if he were dealing cards. He turned the nineteenth fish so the lid of the box would fit properly, keeping the fish fresh while they were transported to town.

20. DRYING SQUID, Hinomisaki, Taisha-chō, Shimane-ken

Squid, when first caught, are translucent for several hours. Drying on bamboo racks in the late afternoon sun, the squid become tough and chewy. They will be marinated in a mixture of soy sauce and *mirin* (a sake derivative), roasted over charcoal, and sold to tourists who visit this dramatic coastal region.

21. FISHING WHARF, Ōhata-chō, Shimokita-gun, Aomori-ken

Fishing is the main industry of the city of Ōhata, at the northern tip of Honshu. Between June and December boats equipped with large electric light bulbs leave the harbor at sunset. In the black of the night, the lights illuminate the sea. The squid, drawn by the light, swim toward the boats and are captured by the fishermen.

22. MAGIC GARDEN, Tsushima-shi, Aichi-ken

This two-hundred-year-old garden is located outside a private home in the historic river town of Tsushima. Unfortunately, this plot of land will be covered with concrete when a highway is built connecting Tsushima and Nagoya. Even though community members protested the loss of this historical property, the city was unable to save it.

In the spring, a pair of swallows living in the entryway of the house were feeding their newly hatched offspring. At night the owner shut the exterior doors, closing the swallows inside. He was awakened each morning at five by their persistent chirping, requesting to be let out.

23. THE WAY OF THE BOW, Engakuji, Kamakura, Kanagawa-ken

Kyūdō (the way of the bow) is better known to westerners as Zen archery. It is considered a form of spiritual training. Practicing the sequence repeatedly improves concentration and creates a sense of spiritual calm. This woman is shooting at a target from a distance of ninety feet. It is the spiritual energy she generates while shooting that is important, not whether she hits the target. She is studying with the aged Zen priest of Engakuji, Oshō Suhara.

24. SHINTO PRIEST, Izumo Taisha, Kitsuki-Higashi, Taisha-chō, Shimane-ken

Izumo Taisha is one of the two most important centers of Shintoism in Japan. The original shrine is believed to have been built during the sixth century. Mr. Fusanori Kitajima is one of two head priests at Izumo Taisha. He is the seventy-ninth generation of his family to serve in this capacity.

Before taking this photograph, I removed distracting background objects, including a framed photograph that was on the shelf. I heard a gasp from the wife of the man who had introduced me to the priest. She was alarmed that I had put a photo of the emperor on the floor, for as a child, she had been taught to worship the photo of the emperor. The priest reached over and placed the photo on a large table, commenting that the emperor visits periodically. The group portrait of himself with the emperor's family was one of his most valued possessions.

25. GIRLS' DAY DOLLS, Ōyama, Tsuruoka-shi, Yamagata-ken

A doctor's family owns this pair of antique porcelain dolls dressed in layered silk kimonos. Their collection of fifty dolls is placed on a stairlike structure in the living room each year to commemorate Girls' Day on the third of March. Girls' Day, which is widely observed in contemporary Japan, celebrates the existence of a girl child in the family. If the dolls are displayed after the first week of March, it is said that the girls of the family will not marry. None of the three daughters of this family is married; the girls jokingly blame the dolls.

26. POTTER'S STUDIO, Odo pottery, Kōchi-shi, Nosayama, Kōchi-ken

These clay canisters are used to hold hot water in the tea ceremony. When the clay is leather-hard, the potter incises a design on the surface and fills it with a light-colored clay. When the containers are completely dry, the refilled area is trimmed to ensure a clear pattern and a uniformly smooth surface. A translucent glaze will be applied to the entire pot.

27. SWIMMING CARP, Yatsuka-chō, Shimane-ken

A wealthy resident of Daikon Shima in southwestern Japan created this garden within the last twenty years. Visitors come in tour buses to view the local tree peonies, to see the garden, and drink ginseng tea, a local product. In Japanese art and literature, carp (koi) symbolize longevity and fortitude. On Boys' Day, May 5, families with young boys celebrate by flying koinobori (cloth streamers made in the shape of a carp) from the rooftops of their homes or the porches of their apartments.

28. LOTUS LEAVES, Shiroishi-chō, Kishima-gun, Saga-ken

Lotus plants, which thrive in marshy areas or paddies, are raised for their exquisite flowers and their large edible roots. After the root is jerked from the sulfurous muck, the eight-foot-tall leaves are cut and left to rot in the water. Lotus roots ripen in midsummer. They are a major product of Kyushu, the southernmost of the four main Japanese islands.

29. AFLOAT, Enokizu, Shinuonome-chō, Minami Matsuura-gun, Nagasaki-ken

Kyushu is known for the quality of its fresh fish. On the islands of Gotō Rettō, an archipelago off the southern coast of Kyushu, fishing is still the primary vocation, but in recent years cooperatives have replaced the solitary fisherman. Boats of this ancient design are propelled and steered by a single person using an oar at the rear of the boat.

Such boats, commonly seen in woodblock prints, are now utilized by the older fishermen of the village to go short distances to bait traps.

30. TIE-DYEING, Arimatsu-chō, Nagoya, Aichi-ken

Arimatsu is one of the shibori (tie-dyeing) centers of Japan. Intricate tying, stitching, and folding methods are used to create complex designs. A single piece of fabric might be retied and immersed in different colors of dyes as many as ten times. Historically the fabrics were used in making kimonos. Since the popularity of kimonos has declined, shibori fabrics are now utilized in contemporary fashion, in door hangings, or in tablecloths.

31. INDIGO DYEING VATS, Kōsei-chō, Shimoda-gun, Shiga-ken

The dyeing master of this house grows his own indigo. He immerses the indigo leaves and stems in these vats to ferment. Over a period of weeks, a progressively more intense color and smell develop. The master carefully evaluates the density of the dye in each vat before submerging his yarns. He and his wife sell the yarns and woven products to people who appreciate the intense blue color that is unique to indigo.

32. GRAPE VINEYARD, Akayama, Kaminoyama-shi, Yamagata-ken

The mountainous regions of Yamagata-ken have rain throughout the summer months. To protect each grape cluster from moisture, a waxlike paper is positioned to act as an umbrella. If the grapes get wet, they begin to rot, and Japanese housewives will not buy them. The appearance of a product is important to the Japanese consumer. Since fruit is often given as a gift to friends or business associates, only flawless fruit is sold. Farmers have adjusted to consumers' perfectionism, but it drives up the cost of Japanese agricultural products.

33. MENDING NETS, Asakawa, Kaifu-gun, Kainan-chō, Tokushima-ken

During the spring, the fishermen leave Asakawa harbor at sunset to lay their nets along the rocky bottom of the shore during the night. Their boats glow with brightly lit bulbs, which attract *ise-ebi* (large shrimp). Before dawn, the nets are hoisted up and the fishermen remove the entangled shrimp. The nets are made of synthetic filament. While the fishermen sleep during the day, their wives or the older people in the village repair the nets.

34. TOBACCO CROP, Torinagane, Ōhasama-chō, Hienuki-gun, Iwate-ken

Tobacco is grown in hilly regions where it is impossible to plant rice. To get the most from his crop, this farmer begins his harvest by cutting the two largest leaves from the bottom of each plant. By harvesting the biggest leaves first and progressively moving up the plant, he gives the smaller leaves more time to grow. In a closed drying tent, he loops a rope around the stem and hangs each leaf individually to dry for forty days.

35. TAILOR'S WINDOW, Tsushima-shi, Aichi-ken

A tailor and his wife operate a two-person business out of their home on a main street of Tsushima, near Nagoya. During the daytime, this room is a tai-

lor's shop. At night they pull futon (bedding) from the large wall cupboards, and the room becomes a bedroom. Like most houses in Japan, this home has little insulation and no central heat. Kerosene space heaters keep the main room warm in the winter.

36. MR. FUJITA AND THE DARUMA SCROLL, Ōhasama-chō, Hienuki-gun, Iwate-ken

Mr. Fujita's most treasured scroll, a Daruma painted by a Buddhist priest named Reikai, is about one hundred years old. The Daruma represents a monk who achieved enlightenment by meditating with such intensity that he lost the use of his arms and legs. Over the years, thousands of artists have painted this subject, but the eyes of Reikai's Daruma are especially alive, setting his work apart.

37. STREET VENDOR'S CART, Takayama-shi, Gifu-ken

Takayama, a picturesque river town, is a popular destination for Japanese tourists. In the historical district, street merchants sell locally made products to visitors. The rice crackers on display here are described by the vendors as *monosugoku umai* (terribly delicious).

38. GATEBALL PLAYERS, Kurokawa, Higashitagawa-gun, Yamagata-ken

The members of this gateball (croquet) team have covered their faces and hands to protect themselves from tanning. The graphite mallets cost $75 apiece, an extravagance for these frugal rural women. But it would be unthinkable to appear at a game with improper equipment. The mallets, made in Japan, bear the English name "Sunrise." Japanese companies commonly use foreign words. English is particularly fashionable, and its use promotes sales in Japan.

39. SHAMISEN IN AN ATTIC, Tsushima-shi, Aichi-ken

The three-stringed *shamisen* has a banjolike sound. The instrument provides background music for puppet and kabuki plays and for some forms of dance. A cat-gut cover is tightly stretched over the base of the instrument. It will rupture if there are dramatic changes in temperature or humidity.

Some young people still study traditional instruments such as the shamisen, but Western instruments — piano and violin — are much more popular.

40. NOH AND KYŌGEN MASKS, Kurokawa, Higashitagawa-gun, Yamagata-ken

During the summer, masks used in noh and kyōgen plays are aired to prevent them from becoming moldy. Most of the masks in this collection are made of cypress, a moisture-resistant wood. They were carved between the sixteenth and nineteenth centuries. The masks cover a male actor's face to make it female, or they allow an actor to make a transition in age or character.

41. YOUNG VISITORS, Kurokawa, Yamagata-ken

An elderly friend invited her neighbor's children to visit her home to meet me, her first foreign guest. But after the initial excitement, they hid behind their drinks and were too shy to talk. Two of the girls are wearing Japanese-made T-shirts on which English words are printed. English words are used as a design element in Japanese fashion, but the phrases are often grammatically incorrect.

42. STRINGS OF PERSIMMONS, Shimoyanagi-mura, Mizusawa-shi, Iwate-ken

In northern Honshu, the *shibugaki* (tart persimmons) ripen at the end of October. Women remove the skins and entwine the stems in twisted strands of rope. For a month, the drying fruit hangs under the eaves to sweeten.

43. SORTING SOYBEANS, Tōno-shi, Iwate-ken

Many farmers still grow enough food in small gardens near their homes to supply their households. Soybeans, an important staple in the Japanese diet, are commonly grown in these vegetable plots. After drying the pods and extracting the soybeans, this woman is removing beans damaged by insects. She might soak and mash the soybeans to make *miso* for soup or marinate them in vinegar to eat as a snack.

44. BROOMS ON A CLAY WALL, Kamegamori, Ōhasama-chō, Hienuki-gun, Iwate-ken

For hundreds of years, walls of homes were constructed by packing a mixture of rice straw, clay, and water onto a bamboo frame. Even now, expensive homes are still built in this traditional manner. The clay absorbs the humidity in the summer, making the homes cool and comfortable. In the winter, clay walls retain the heat. This ninety-year-old wall is gradually deteriorating from lack of repair.

45. BACKLIT RADISHES, Kamega-mori, Ōhasama-chō, Hienuki-gun, Iwate-ken

During the fall, long white *daikon* radishes are pulled from the earth to hang on bamboo poles to dry. In this region, after drying for two weeks, the radishes are placed in salt and *nuka* (the bran of rice) and pressed under weight for about one month. The resulting *tsukemono*, a salty appetizer, can be stored without refrigeration.

46. RICE HARVEST, Ishidoriya-chō, Iwate-ken

In early fall, farmers drain and weed their rice paddies. In late September, they cut the rice and hang it from bamboo poles for several weeks. When dry, they push the stalks through a threshing machine, which separates the grain from the chaff.

47. EIGHTY-YEAR-OLD FARMER, Shiroishi-chō, Kishima-gun, Saga-ken

This elderly farmer offered to pose in the rain outfit he wore as a young man. The hat, made from the exterior covering of the bamboo shoot, is water-repellent. Raincoat designs vary throughout Japan (see plate 56). This design, common in Kyushu in the pre-war period, is now almost never used.

48. TEA CEREMONY KETTLES, Morioka-shi, Iwate-ken

Like their clay counterparts (plate 26), cast iron kettles are used to hold hot water in the tea ceremony. Made in the Suzuki studio in Morioka, the pots were cast in a clay and plaster mold that is used once and then discarded. The tiny indentations in the mold (bottom left), made dot by dot with a pointed hand tool, become textural protrusions in the metal container.

49. BAMBOO WHISKS, Takayama-chō, Ikoma-shi, Nara-ken

Chasen have just one function — they are whisks in the tea ceremony. The craft of whisk-making has existed unchanged for five hundred years. Mr. Toshiyuki Hirata, who learned this craft from his father, expects to spend his whole life perfecting his craft. Mr. Hirata uses three-year-old bamboo, which he first bleaches and then dries for approximately a year. The whitened bamboo is cut into 4 1/2-inch sections. In an intricate process, it is subsequently cut into 160 slices, an inner and an outer ring, each 1/32 of an inch in thickness.

50. SHIITAKE LOGS IN WINTER, Ōhasama-chō, Hienuki-gun, Iwate-ken

Shiitake mushrooms are a delicacy in Japanese cooking. In recent years, to accommodate the demand, shiitake farmers select a shady, moist spot in which to stack oak logs. They drill holes in the logs and inject shiitake spores. Within a year or two, the aged logs will be covered with mushrooms.

51. WATAMUKI SHRINE, Hino-chō, Shiga-ken

When friends took me to the Watamuki Shrine, for fun, we purchased *omikuji* (fortunes) for a donation of 100 yen (75 cents). Mine predicted bad luck, and my friends refused to read it out loud. On their advice, I tied it to a tree and purchased another, trying to improve my fate. Later, while exploring the shrine, I slipped on a bridge and banged my camera on the stone walkway, cracking a filter. When I looked up, my friends were smiling and chattering, relieved that my portended bad luck was over.

The horse in the photograph was painted 175 years ago as a gift to the gods.

52. POND IN WINTER, Haguro, Yamagata-ken

In this peaceful scene, three trees are growing — *sakura* (cherry), *matsu* (pine), and *take* (bamboo). In Japanese art and literature, the cherry symbolizes the transience of life since the blossoms fall in midbloom; the pine denotes long life because it is an evergreen; the bamboo represents straightforwardness and tenacity because it grows upright in mountainous terrain. During the winter, fragile trees and bushes are supported with wooden structures or wrapped with straw mats to prevent the accumulation of heavy snow. The loss of a single branch in a heavy storm could change the balance of the whole garden.

53. EIGHT FOLLOWERS OF BUD-DHA, Chōshōji, Hirosaki-shi, Aomori-ken

Sets of the Five Hundred Followers of Buddha, called Gohyaku Rakan, are displayed in various temples throughout Japan. This collection is unusual since it has one hundred, not five hundred, statues. No one is certain what happened to the missing figures.

The road that leads to Chōshōji is lined with ancient temples, many in various states of disrepair.

54. TEMPLE OF CARVED STONES, Ishidō-ji, Gamō-chō, Shiga-ken

Ishidō-ji is one of the oldest temples in central Japan. According to historical records, it was established by Korean monks at the end of the seventh century. The figures on the surface of these stones were carved in the thirteenth century to honor the memory of ancestors.

55. MOUNTAIN VILLAGE, Asahi-mura, Aza-Tamugimata, Yamagata-ken

The mountains near Asahi-mura receive some of the heaviest snows in Japan. During the day, skiers traverse the slopes in a popular ski area nearby. At night, some choose to stay in a three-story thatched home in this village. Because of the overwhelming expense of upkeep, homes with thatched roofs are becoming rare. Owners cover the old roofs with corrugated sheets of metal to keep them from leaking, or they replace them with tile. Throughout the village an extensive network of concrete canals brings fresh water in and prevents the melting snow from causing erosion.

56. WALKING HOME IN THE SNOW, Kurokawa, Higashitagawa-gun, Yamagata-ken

Occasionally women in this region still wear raincoats (*mino*) of this design to protect themselves from rain and snow. Made of rice straw (*wara*), the raincoats are at least fifty years old. With the introduction of modern water-repellent materials, straw raincoats are now crafted only for dolls.

57. SNOW-COVERED ROOFTOP,
Kurokawa, Higashitagawa-gun,
Yamagata-ken

Historically, thatched roofs in
Yamagata-ken were constructed with a
steep pitch. They are solidly reinforced
by crossbeams, so they can support the
heavy accumulation of snow that comes
each winter to this region. The roof pic-
tured here is part of a shrine at the base
of a steep hill. Each summer damaged
sections of the roof must be rethatched.

The negatives for these photographs were made with a four-by-five-inch Wista view camera and with a Pentax 645 using T-Max 100 and T-Max 400 film. The originals were printed on Portriga Rapid paper (111 surface) and toned in selenium. Exposure times ranged from one-sixtieth of a second to fifteen minutes.

The typefaces used in this book are Centaur and Arrighi. Centaur is a modern face based on the original work of Bruce Rogers in 1914. It was based on the roman letter used by the type designer, Jenson, for his Eusebius, one of the most beautiful types of the fifteenth century. The elegant italic, Arrighi, was designed by Frederic Warde in 1925 to accompany Centaur. The calligraphic quality of the letterforms suggests the delicateness of Japanese kanji characters.

This book was designed by Janice Wheeler for the Smithsonian Institution Press and typeset by Graphic Composition in Athens, Georgia.

The book was printed on one-hundred-pound Quintessence dull text by the Stinehour Press in Lunenberg, Vermont.